FACTOLOGY
SHARKS

Open up a world of information!

READ THE REAL SHARK STORY

This book was 540 million years in the making! Sharks (or elasmobranch fish if we're being scientific) are among the oldest living things on Earth. They've been cruising the deep since before the seven continents were formed. Five mass extinctions may have wiped many species from the face of the planet but somehow sharks have survived them all and remained on top of the ocean's food chain.

Maybe that – and the classic action-adventure thriller *Jaws* – is why many people find sharks so frightening. But the truth is that very few of them are a danger to humans and, as you're about to find out, there is so much more to sharks that makes them some of the most amazing creatures in the world.

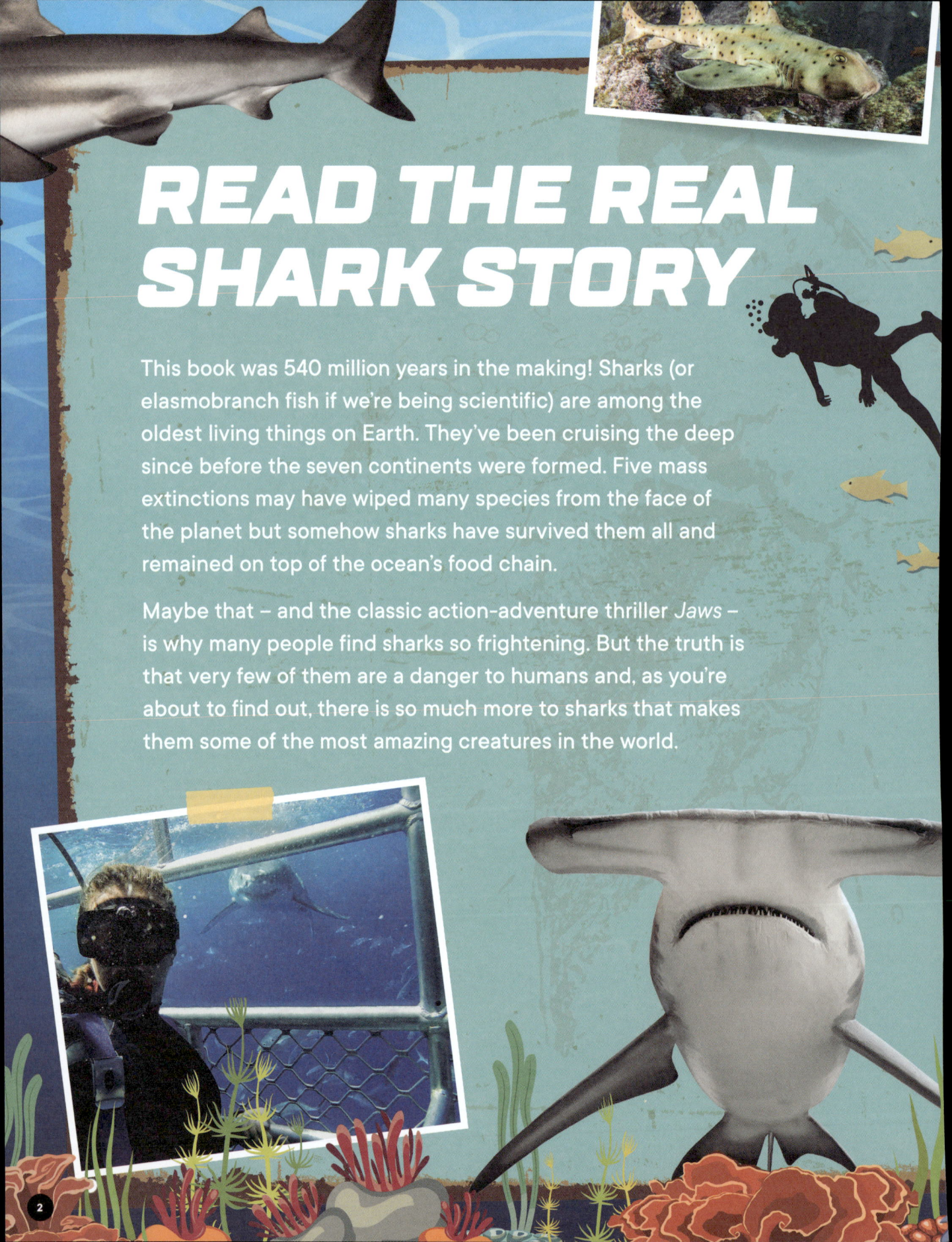

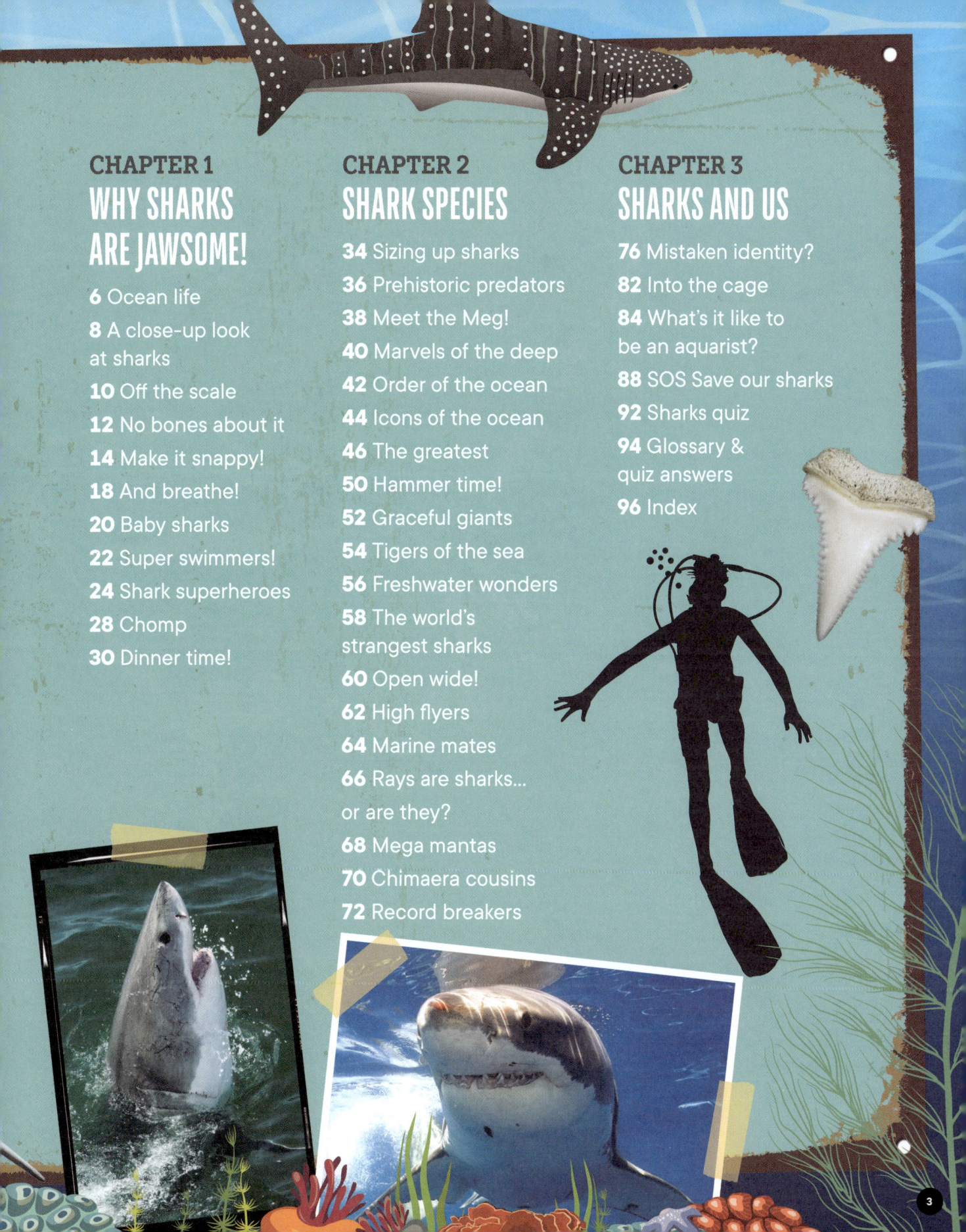

CHAPTER 1
WHY SHARKS ARE JAWSOME!

CHAPTER 2
SHARK SPECIES

CHAPTER 3
SHARKS AND US

CHAPTER 1
WHY SHARKS ARE JAWSOME!

Bendy skeletons, sensitive snouts, big brains and ridiculous teeth are just a few of the many reasons why it's sharks that rule the waves....

Sharks are a special type of fish! Find out what sets them apart from the other creatures who share their...

OCEAN LIFE

ZEBRA SHARK

What exactly is a shark?

Sharks are some of the coolest dudes in the ocean. They belong to a group of fish called chondrichthyes. Rays and skates also belong to this bunch, who all have skeletons made of bendy cartilage. Sharks don't have lungs like mammals do, but still need oxygen to survive. They get this by absorbing oxygen from the water using their gills.

WHALE SHARK

BLUE SHARK

BLUE SPOTTED RAY

SPOTTED EAGLE RAY

SOUTHERN STINGRAY

MARINE MAMMALS

These guys spend most of their time living in or near the ocean. Just like land-loving mammals, they breathe air through their lungs, have hair and feed their young on milk. Let's take a look at some of the different types...

HARP SEAL

Cetaceans

Cetaceans are completely aquatic. This means they spend all their time in the water but need to come up to the surface to breathe air. Whales, dolphins and porpoises are all cetaceans.

HUMPBACK WHALE

ORCA

COMMON DOLPHIN

Pinnipeds

Seals, sea lions and walruses all belong to the pinniped group of mammals. These mammals can live in the ocean but also like spending a lot of time on land. Pinnipeds have front and back flippers to help them move through the water.

WALRUS

SPOTTED SEAL

Bony fish

Osteichthyes (or bony fish) have skeletons made of bone. Familiar faces such as salmon and tuna are among their ranks, as are the tropical species clown fish and angelfish. Approximately 95% of fish in the world's oceans are bony!

Sea turtles

Sea turtles are cold-blooded reptiles. This means they lay eggs, have scaly skin and breathe in air. There are seven types of sea turtle in the world's seas. Like sharks, sea turtles are one of the oldest creatures on the planet and have survived for around 110 million years. They spend much of their life swimming in water but lay their eggs on land.

MUSSELS

SCALLOP

SPINY ROCK LOBSTER

BLUE CRAB

Shellfish

Even though they live in the water, shellfish aren't fish! The term refers to any marine invertebrate (animal without a backbone) that has a shell. Shellfish are split into two groups. The first is molluscs, which usually have hinged shells and soft bodies and count oysters, mussels, scallops and clams among their number. Second are crustaceans, such as crabs, prawns and lobsters, which all have jointed legs and hard shells.

SEA TURTLE

Sirenians

Manatees and dugongs are sirenians. This is the only group of marine mammals whose members don't eat meat. Due to their veggie diet, sirenians can usually be found in shallow waters that are full of plants to snack on.

POLAR BEAR

MANATEE

Marine fissipeds

Marine fissipeds are mammals who spend most of their time on land but love taking a dip in the ocean when it's time for dinner. Polar bears and sea otters both belong in this gang.

SEA OTTER

A CLOSE-UP LOOK AT SHARKS

It's time to strap on your snorkel and flippers and take a deep dive into the incredible workings of the shark's body

Ampullae of Lorenzini on the snout of a shortfin mako shark

SNOUT

A shark's snout is covered in small pores called 'ampullae of Lorenzini'! These impressive-sounding dots can detect even the smallest electrical currents given off by prey swimming in the water.

GILLS

Sharks use their gills to breathe. As they swim forward, water enters their mouth and exits out of the gills.

BRAIN

Sharks have bigger brains for their size than most other fish. The great white's brain is Y-shaped with two bulbs at the end!

TEETH

The most legendary part of a shark has got to be those pearly whites. All that chomping on prey makes a shark's triangular, blade-like teeth wear down. Unlike humans, who head to the dentist, sharks simply replace them!

STOMACH

Shaped like the letter 'J', the stomach can stretch to make room for bigger meals and – look away now! – even turtles, seals and dolphins. Carnivorous sharks can swallow their prey whole. Planktivorous sharks feed on plankton, which are tiny organisms carried along by the tide.

PECTORAL FINS

There are two of these steering fins, one on either side. They are which are like aeroplane wings. Instead of air, water lifts the shark up, up... and away!

TEETHING'S A PROBLEM FOR HUMANS, BUT NOT FOR ME!

▲ Baby whitetip shark

DORSAL FIN

Tough rope-like fibres inside the fin stiffen and relax to stop the shark rolling all over the place and keep it swimming in a straight line.

CAUDAL FIN

Have you used flippers to power you through the sea? That's what a shark uses this fin – or tail – for!

TRUE or FALSE?

Some shark species can push their stomachs out through their mouths and give it a quick wash to get rid of anything nasty!

TRUE ☐   FALSE ☐

ANSWER: TRUE!

MUSCLE

Sharks have two types of muscle – red and white!
- White muscle powers short fast sprints – towards prey or to escape danger.
- Red muscle is fuelled by fat for longer swims across the ocean.

LIVER

Hogging up to 90% of the shark's internal space, the liver is a huge floating aid.

Like water wings, it keeps the fish in perfect neutral buoyancy, so it doesn't float or sink. It's also an energy store, topped up with oils and fatty acids.

SPIRAL VALVE

A shark's supper gets digested in a part of the small intestine known as the spiral valve.

DID YOU know?

A great white shark's liver weighs around **465KG**. That's about **10 TIMES HEAVIER** than you are!

OFF THE SCALE

It's not just a shark's mouth that's full of teeth – their skin is, too! If you ever get close enough to feel the skin of a shark, you might be surprised at its texture

Feeling rough

If you were to touch a shark's skin, you'd notice something unusual. Stroke it forwards – towards the nose – and it feels rough, like sandpaper. But stroked the other way, towards the tail, it feels smooth.

It's because shark skin is made up of millions of tiny scales called denticles. These denticles look exactly like teeth and have the same construction, with a hard, enamel-like covering over a layer of dentine on top of a soft pulp cavity.

Go with the flow

When it comes to swimming, a shark's amazing skin gives it a big advantage. As the shark swims, each scale creates a tiny swirl (or vortex) in the water, making a cushioning layer around the shark that lets it slip very easily through the sea. Different types of shark have different-shaped denticles – some increase their speed, others increase their ability to turn in the water.

EXCITING EVOLUTION

Experts have found connections between the shape of a shark's scales and the way it lives. Sharks living near reefs, such as gulper sharks, have smooth scales to protect them from injuries against rocks. Great whites and hammerheads, on the other hand, have special extra ridges on their scales that reduce drag and enable them to swim faster using the same amount of energy.

The swift-swimming hammerhead shark

The nurse shark's smoother denticles make a great shield

DENTICLES ARE TINY!
THEY VARY IN SIZE FROM
0.001MM TO 1MM

BLACKTIP REEF SHARK DENTICLES

Strong shield

Denticles don't increase in size as the shark does, but more scales are grown to fill in the gaps – much like adding links to chain mail – and replace those the shark has already shed. Denticles are hardcore! They act as a protective armour, preventing sharks from being scratched. Some bottom-feeders have tough shield-like scales on their bellies to protect them from the rough seabed while they're feeding.

The shape of sharks' scales makes it harder for harmful microbes and parasites to latch on and grow.

SWIM SCIENCE

Shark skin is so energy-efficient, researchers recreated its qualities for everything from boats and cars to swimsuits. In fact, some shark-inspired swimsuits are so effective they've been banned from competitions!

TRUE or FALSE?

In the past, shark skin was actually used as sandpaper!

TRUE ☐ FALSE ☐

ANSWER: TRUE. Known as shagreen, shark skin was used in carpentry to smooth wood before sandpaper was invented.

NO BONES ABOUT IT

Sharks don't have any bones. Their skeletons are made from the same bendy stuff as your ears and nose – just stronger!

GILL ARCHES

These cartilage loops support the gills and hold them in place.

WATERY SUPPORT

Shark skeletons can be more flexible than ours because they live in water, which supports their bodies. As sharks get older, their skeletons get harder.

JAWS

Cleverly, a shark's powerful jaws are not attached to the skull. They're flexible and sometimes extendable, allowing species such as the goblin shark to move its jaws independently to – snap! – snare prey.

Flexible fish

Most fish are famously full of bones, but sharks don't have any. Like rays and skates, the shark is what is known as an elasmobranch, which means its skeleton is made from cartilage.

Press the top rim of your ear between your thumb and first finger – that's cartilage. Do you feel how bendy it is?

Sharks use this flexibility to brilliant effect in the water, switching direction in a split second. And it's so light that it helps them stay afloat, too!

FAST FACT

The growth bands (rings) on the individual bones of a shark's spine grow in pairs and alternate between opaque and translucent.

DORSAL FIN

The inside of a shark's dorsal fin has cartilage rods to support it, making it rigid. Some species – such as the dogfish and Port Jackson shark – have even developed spines on their dorsal fins that can secrete venom!

A spiny dogfish's venomous spike

There's no science to back it up, but certain cultures still use shark cartilage to cure arthritis and cancer

BACKBONE

Sharks are vertebrates, meaning they have spines – although these are made from cartilage, too. A great white shark can have between 170 to 187 vertebrae. Compare that with the 33 knobbly vertebrae humans have and you get a sense of the vast size of these magnificently bendy beasts!

FLEXIBLE   STRONG

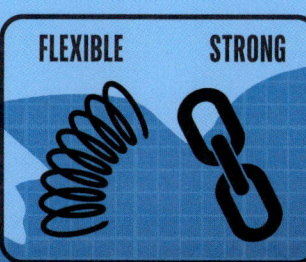

Bone benefits

Today there are around 1,000 species of fish with skeletons made of cartilage, but more than 28,000 with mostly bony skeletons. Bone doesn't bend and must be strong enough to support muscles working well. Bony bodies evolved in lots of different ways, giving such fish more scope to adapt how they move through the water. Bony fish became amphibians, who were the first creatures to crawl out of the sea and live on land. These in turn gave rise to reptiles, and from them came birds and mammals. This means we can trace our brilliant bony bodies all the way back to some very ancient fish!

EVOLVE *and* ADAPT

Fossils suggest sharks had bones around 250 million years ago, before evolving into the bendy cartilaginous fish we know today.

 As well as being lighter and more flexible, cartilage is weaker than bone. So sharks had to develop a thicker skin to protect themselves!

 Having flexible jaws made from cartilage meant sharks could open their mouths wider, which gave them a far more powerful bite.

 Unlike bone, cartilage doesn't ever stop growing. This gave sharks the chance to develop into some of the ocean's biggest predators.

Sharks may not have a bony skeleton, but they more than make up for it with their marvellous mouthful of teeth! Why are they so special? Time to feast on some facts!

MAKE IT SNAPPY!

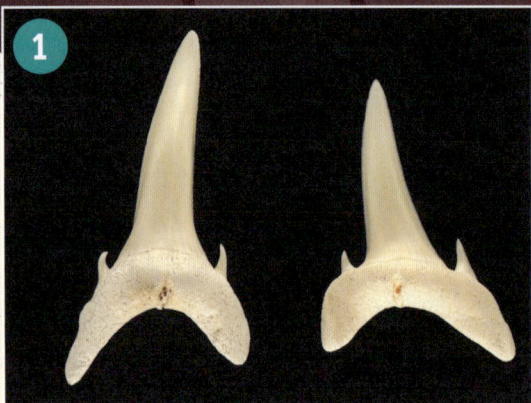

1

LONG, NARROW TEETH

These needle-like gnashers help speedy shark species grip down on slippery fish so they don't get away – a bit like a trap in the wild!

2

PLATE-LIKE TEETH

Perfect for sharks close to the seabed, plate-like teeth are great for crushing and grinding crustacean and mollusc shells. Cracking!

TYPES OF TEETH
There are four main types of teeth among sharks and they suit all 500+ species' style of snacking.

SHARP AND SERRATED TEETH

Great whites and tiger sharks need heavy-duty teeth to slice and dice their food. The bigger the teeth... the bigger the meal!

THE TINIEST TEETH

Whale sharks have thousands of teeth, and they're each about the size of a matchstick head. As you'll see, they're not used for eating at all.

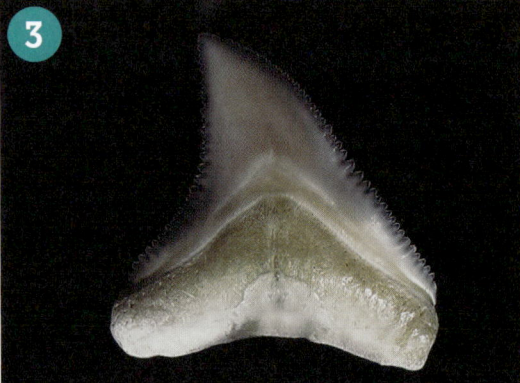

3

4

TIGER SHARK
up to 5cm

BULL SHARK
up to 3cm

LEMON SHARK
up to 2cm

SAND TIGER SHARK
up to 2.5cm

GREAT WHITE SHARK
up to 6.5cm

Rows that grow

Unlike us, sharks continuously shed their teeth throughout their lifetime, and it's thought that some species from the ground shark family can get through 40,000. Compared to adult humans (who usually have 32 teeth) sharks have a system a little like a conveyor belt. Their teeth never stop growing and rotating forwards. This means that no matter how they decide to dine, a shark's dentures are *always* super-strong.

EXPERIMENT

- 🟥 INCISORS
- 🟦 CANINE
- 🟩 PREMOLAR
- 🟧 MOLAR

TOOTH TEST

For the next three days, write a list of everything you eat, and pay attention to which teeth you're using. Humans have four types of teeth, and they're not all used for chewing. What have you learnt about your canine, incisor, molar, and premolar teeth?

Which teeth in your mouth match the descriptions of shark teeth?

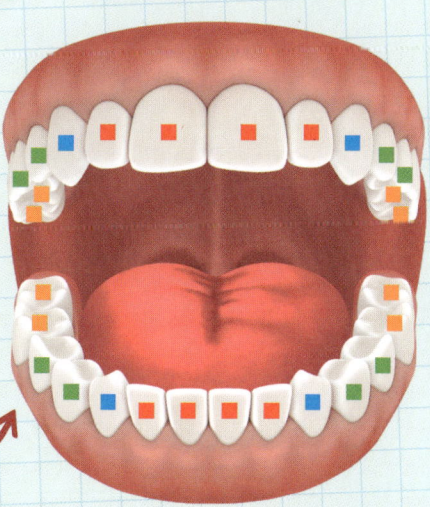

FAST⚡FACT

The warmth of the water affects *so much* of a shark's physiology, including how often its teeth regrow. Scientists found that nurse sharks' teeth grow slower when it's cold.

Wonky teeth? Wanna say it to my face?

Shortfin mako shark

Messy munchers

Why do some sharks' teeth look so terrifying? Sand tiger sharks are known as ragged-tooth sharks in South Africa, and it's no wonder... they're all over the place! The jaws of the shortfin mako and tiger shark are so much more flexible than humans – this helps to withstand the impact of feeding at high speed. All that wear and tear might make some sharks' teeth a bit wonky, but such messy mouths mean that prey won't get away – if even only caught by the tip!

A tiger shark's mangled mouth

PEARLY WHITES

By continuously regrowing their teeth, sharks keep their pearly whites permanently sharp and free from painful cavities. Sharks don't have dentists, but then their teeth are never around for long enough to need a check-up. Scientists have recently found that certain species even have a layer of pure fluoride on their teeth, which is the same natural mineral used to protect enamel in most toothpastes.

Steak knife spikes

When our food's on a plate, we have different tools to cut it up. Just look at a steak knife compared to a normal table knife – it's spiky, with serrated sides like a saw. Humans have canine, incisor, molar and premolar teeth and they're all adapted to do different jobs. Sharks' teeth, on the other fin, are multi-purpose to suit their eating style. Tiger shark spikes hold prey in place, while their serrated sides cut it up. That's gotta hurt!

FACT EVEN IF SHARKS' TEETH LOOK SIMILAR, DIFFERENT SPECIES EAT DIFFERENTLY. **MAKO SHARKS** RIP FLESH OFF FISH, WHEREAS **TIGER SHARKS** TAKE MUCH NEATER BITES.

QUITE A MOUTHFUL

Some sharks don't even use their teeth at all when they're eating! In order to eat, basking sharks keep their mouths wide open while they swim, swallowing plankton and small fish whole.

FACT UNLIKE MEGAMOUTH SHARKS, **BASKING SHARKS** DON'T EVEN NEED TO SUCK WATER IN TO CHOW DOWN. THEY JUST KEEP SWIMMING TOWARDS FOOD!

That's just swell

The swell shark's teeth look a lot like Velcro! Although it's a hunter, the swell shark prefers to go on the defensive, and will swallow water to puff up its body and scare off would-be attackers. So, what does it need its teeth for? For its size, the swell shark's mouth is wider than a great white's. It sucks up crustaceans, molluscs and tiny reef fish before snapping its mouth shut behind them.

FAST⚡FACT

What makes **shark teeth so strong?** Their enamel is mostly made up of calcium phosphate. This is the **hardest biological material** inside humans and sharks.

AND BREATHE!

Like humans, sharks need oxygen to stay alive. There's way more oxygen in the air than in the waters they call home, but sharks have a pretty awesome built-in system to breathe in as much as they can. Phew! Time to take a deep breath...

WHAT, NO LUNGS?

● OXYGENATED BLOOD TO BODY VIA HEART
● DE-OXYGENATED BLOOD TO GILLS

EXCESS WATER AND CO_2 PUSHED OUT OF GILLS

WATER PASSES OVER GILLS, WHICH EXTRACT OXYGEN

2

1 OXYGEN-RICH WATER SUCKED IN THROUGH MOUTH

3

HEART

SPIRACLE

SPIRACLE

Gills

Most sharks have five pairs of flap-like slits, which open and close, on either side of their heads. They're known as gills and are the main gatherers of oxygen.

RAM VENTILATION

1 The simple action of swimming and moving through the ocean is enough for most sharks to get the oxygen they need. As water flows over the gills, tiny thread-like blood vessels absorb the oxygen into the shark's bloodstream. This is called ram ventilation and basking sharks and hammerhead sharks are two species that breathe like this.

2 The blood is whisked around the shark's body to the heart before returning to the gills.

3 Just as the gills filter healthy oxygen, they also rid the shark of waste carbon dioxide. And then the process starts all over again!

Catching some Zzzs

Scientists spent a long time puzzling over whether ram ventilator sharks would die if they stopped swimming. It turns out they do something called sleep swimming! How is that possible? The shark's spinal cord coordinates its swimming movements, which allows the brain to switch off and get some much-needed shut-eye.

#Sharkgoals

The small-spotted catshark is one of several species that can lie on the seabed and breathe without swimming. They suck the water into their mouths, using large – and strong! – cheek muscles to squirt it over their gills in a process called buccal pumping.

Yo-yo swimming

Another way sharks conserve energy is by swimming to the surface of the ocean before completely relaxing and chilling out on the descent. Great white sharks making the long migration – an annual trip between Australia and South Africa – are yo-yoing champions!

It's tactical!

Just as you hold your breath when diving underwater so you don't waste oxygen, the epaulette shark does a similar thing in the shallow waters. There it holds onto its oxygen supplies by lowering its energy output.

WATCH OUT, SHARK ABOUT!

A shark's prey radar is always on high alert, even when it's sleep swimming! Nemo, you have been warned...

HEY! WHO ARE YOU CALLING 'TOTALLY DOTTY'?

DID YOU know?

Some sharks **glow in the dark**. It's a way of communicating!

SPIRACLE

Miracle spiracle

Like most sharks, the totally dotty horn shark has evolved a tiny opening behind each eye. They're called spiracles, and they suck water in when the shark is lying on the ocean floor just waiting to pounce on unsuspecting prey. The sea floor-dwelling cousins of sharks – rays and skates – have them too because their gills are underneath their bodies. Spiracles work like a snorkel to suck oxygen-rich water over the gills.

Deep dive

The shortfin mako scours low-oxygen areas in search of a tasty snack. That's the equivalent of humans going for a fast sprint, so these sharks need some serious recovery time afterwards.

BABY SHARKS

If all that comes to mind when you hear the words 'baby shark' is a catchy song on YouTube, then it's time to get PUP-to-date with the earliest stage of a shark's life

HOW DO SHARKS GIVE BIRTH?

Giving birth is no simple matter for sharks. Some lay eggs, some give birth to live sharks and some babies even eat their brothers and sisters to survive. Why? Let's find out!

1 VIVIPARITY →

Just like mammals, viviparous sharks give birth to live shark pups. The shark embryo (a baby shark that is just starting to develop) is surrounded inside its mother by a yolk sac placenta. The future pup receives all the nutrients it needs to grow big and strong through the placenta. The number of shark pups a viviparous shark can give birth to varies from between two and 20. Some scientists have even found pregnant whale sharks that are carrying nearly 300 pups inside! Lemon sharks, blue sharks, silvertip sharks and hammerheads are just some of the species that give birth to their young. Welcome, little ones!

> **FACT** THE GREENEYE DOGFISH SHARK CAN BE **PREGNANT** FOR **THREE YEARS**

2 OVOVIVIPARITY ←

Ovoviviparity is perhaps the strangest way some sharks give birth. The female doesn't lay eggs – instead, they hatch and develop inside her until they're ready to be born. In some shark species, the pups live inside the mother and feed off unfertilised eggs and sometimes even eat siblings. Isn't that wild? Cookiecutter, great white, nurse, pygmy and tiger sharks are all ovoviviparous.

3 OVIPARITY →

Unlike viviparous sharks, oviparous sharks lay eggs in the ocean. Some females carry their eggs in their mouth until they find a safe place to leave them, while others spend hours laying their eggs to make sure they are secure on the seabed. Just like the eggs you have for breakfast, a shark's egg has a yolk too, which is where baby sharks get all the tasty nutrients they need to grow. Once fully developed, the little shark will chew its way out of the egg case and swim off. Most species of shark are oviparous, including the zebra, cat and horn shark.

FACT RATS AND LEMURS HAVE PUPS TOO!

FACT SHARKS DON'T NEED TO BREASTFEED. SOME SPECIES **MAKE MILK IN THE UTERUS**.

Mermaid's purse

A mermaid's purse is the name given to the tough, leather-looking capsule that a shark's embryo grows inside. These cool cases protect the growing baby shark until they're ready to hatch and contain a yolk sac. Empty egg cases wash up on shorelines all around the world. Scientists can tell which species of shark each egg case belongs to just by studying its size, shape and features.

FAST⚡FACT

Some egg cases have long threadlike tendrils hanging down, which attach to the seabed. These tendrils keep the egg cases together and stop the ocean's current washing them away.

Bullhead sharks' eggs are spiral in shape. They place their eggs in between rocks, where the spiral shape helps keep it safe and wedged in place.

Super SWIMMERS!

Sharks come in many shapes and sizes, but they all share certain features that propel them through water with ease

JET-PROPELLED

If many modern fighter jets look shark-like, it's because they use similar features to move through the air in the same way that sharks swim through the water. Sharks that swim in the ocean all have a similar teardrop-style body that's larger at the front and thins out at the end. This shape is known as thunniform ('tuna-like') because it resembles a tunafish. It enables sharks who have this body type (such as the great white and mako) to swim fast for long periods. Other sharks have an anguilliform (or 'eel-like') shape and swim in an 'S' pattern just like eels or snakes do.

UPPER LOBE

LOWER LOBE

TAIL ENGINE

All sharks have a big tail that propels them through the water. The larger the tail, the faster the shark. It usually comes in two shapes:

* The **HOMOCERCAL**, which has an upper and lower lobe of roughly the same size. This shape is ideal for swimming at speed and is seen on the fastest of sharks such as the mako.

* The **HETEROCERCAL**, which has unequal lobes. The upper one is larger (in some cases, much larger) than the lower one. This shape is ideal for slow-swimming sharks who travel long distances. The power generated by the movement of the upper lobe pushes the tail down and the nose up, keeping the shark level.

EVEN KEEL

In some sharks there's a raised ridge on either side of the tail where it meets the body. This is called the caudal keel, which strengthens the tail to make it more powerful. It also helps streamline the shark, so it can move more easily through water.

FAST FIN

Despite apparently being designed to terrify swimmers on the cinema screen, the dorsal fin actually keeps the shark stable in the water and stops it rolling over. When sharks swim fast, the dorsal fin stiffens to provide more stability at higher speeds. In sharks that hunt near reefs and need to turn rapidly, the fin is flexible to help them manoeuvre.

FAST ⚡ FACT

Sharks can't move their pectoral fins like paddles the way bony fish do, so they **can't swim backwards!**

FLYING UNDERWATER

The jet and the shark also have 'wings' in common. In the case of the shark, two large pectoral fins just behind and beneath the head generate 'lift' as the shark moves forward, stopping it from sinking. These work in the same way as birds' wings do when they fly. In some sharks and rays, these pectoral fins have evolved into actual wing shapes that are used to 'fly' through the water.

FULL STEAM AHEAD!

It's tricky to measure how fast sharks can swim, because they snake about in the water. Most travel at a chilled 2.5km/h. But if they're after food, they sure put on a spurt!

0   10   20   30   40   50   60   70   80

Mako shark
48–74km/h

Great white shark
40–56km/h

39km/h

Blue shark

Olympic swimmer
8km/h

SHARK SUPERHEROES

Sensing electricity! Seeing in the dark! Smelling in stereo?! Sharks spent hundreds of millions of years evolving these superpowers so they could become the underwater Avengers we know today

Marine magic

Here's one superpower humans definitely don't have! Chimaeras, rays, sharks (and even sturgeon fish) have special mucus-filled pores called ampullae of Lorenzini. These incredible spots are related to the shark's lateral line, and allow species to 'electro sense' – detect the heartbeats and movement of their prey. Scientists think sharks use these gooey tubes to feel temperature and changes in water pressure, too.

A tiger shark's mega sensors... not freckles!

Smelling in the sea

How do sharks smell in the sea if we can't? Nestled in a shark's nose are its nares, which are organs used exclusively for smelling (not breathing).

There's a myth that sharks can smell blood from kilometres away... but this isn't strictly true! Scents reach sharks through currents – so, in the same way humans pick up scents on the breeze, the motion of the ocean plays its part. If water's waving in the right direction, they can smell the length of three football fields!

Sharks have sensory cells called olfactory lamellae. These have refined as sharks evolved to detect chemical changes in the water, which are caused by anything from algae to fish wee – not just blood. So, in this way, their sense of smell works like a breadcrumb trail.

FACT SHARKS **DON'T GO CRAZY** WHEN THEY **SMELL BLOOD**, BUT THEY ARE ATTRACTED TO IT. THEY **PREFER THE PONG** OF FISH BLOOD TO COW'S BLOOD. THAT'S LUCKY FOR LANDLUBBERS LIKE THEM AND US!

NARES

EAR

Ear, there and everywhere

Some humans struggle when they get water in their ears, but sharks don't have to worry about swimmer's ear! They don't have sticky-outy ears like ours, but sharks do have an inner ear. On a great white's head, you'll see two small holes. More so than any other super-sense, their hearing might be the first sign that prey is passing by! Sound travels faster and further underwater, so sharks can pick up different activity around them in the ocean. They can hear a fin drop!

Seabed sonar

Sharks have a secret sixth sense, and it lets them turn their own body into a radar. The lateral line is a collection of small pores that runs all the way from the snout to the tip of the tail. Like the sensitive nerves in our skin, these holes pick up tiny changes in the water and give sharks a special spatial awareness. When sharks waft their fins, they're able to make waves and bounce them off nearby objects.

LATERAL LINE

Tiger sharks have a third eyelid, just like cats

SHARK EYES

Eye protection

When certain species strike, their eyes go white! As the tiger shark attacks, it rolls its eyes back in its sockets, revealing the white surface of the eyeball. This protects the delicate front section of the eye from getting scratched up. Some species even have a third eyelid known as a nictitating membrane, which fully guards it from rubbish. Sharks' pupils are just like ours – they grow wider to let more light in.

ACTIVITY

Floating fins

Grab a bottle of cooking oil and ask an adult to help you draw a shark's mouth, gills and fins on it with a marker. Fill a sink with water and place your sharky bottle in your temporary tank. You'll see that it floats! Unlike bony fish, sharks don't have an air-filled swim bladder. Oil is lighter than water, and their oil-filled livers are more buoyant than the water around them. With no air in their bodies, sharks can swim past sonar detectors without setting them off!

Out for the count

Want to get really close to a shark? Turn it upside down! Species including tiger sharks can suffer from a curious condition called tonic immobility when they're turned on their head. Why? Scientists think it has something to do with mating in female members of the species – the dorsal fins straighten out and their breathing gets heavy. Have you ever seen an upside-down shark in the wild? We haven't!

FACT IT TAKES UP TO **15 MINUTES** FOR TIGER SHARKS TO **RISE AND SHINE** FOLLOWING TONIC IMMOBILITY. WAKEY, WAKEY!

TONIC IMMOBILITY

Crystal clear sight

Ever opened your eyes underwater? Human eyes are designed to see through the air, with no obstruction. We rely on our eye lenses to refract the light in front of us. Sharks eyes are quite similar to human eyes in that they have a cornea, an iris, lens, pupil and a retina. Recent studies show that some species can even see in colour, too.

What really makes them stand out is a reflective layer of crystals known as the tapetum lucidum, which might sound like a wizard's spell but isn't magic! They've been swimming in the dark for so long, they've developed it to boost the light delivered to the retina. Cats, deer, ferrets and horses also have this shiny layer, which is why their eyes all reflect light.

Shark eyes use water like glasses to focus. Twice the light means they can see up to 10 times better than humans in the water, whether it's murky, dark or clear.

FACT MOST SHARKS CAN **SEE 15-30M AHEAD**, DEPENDING ON THE MURKINESS OF THE OCEAN AROUND THEM.

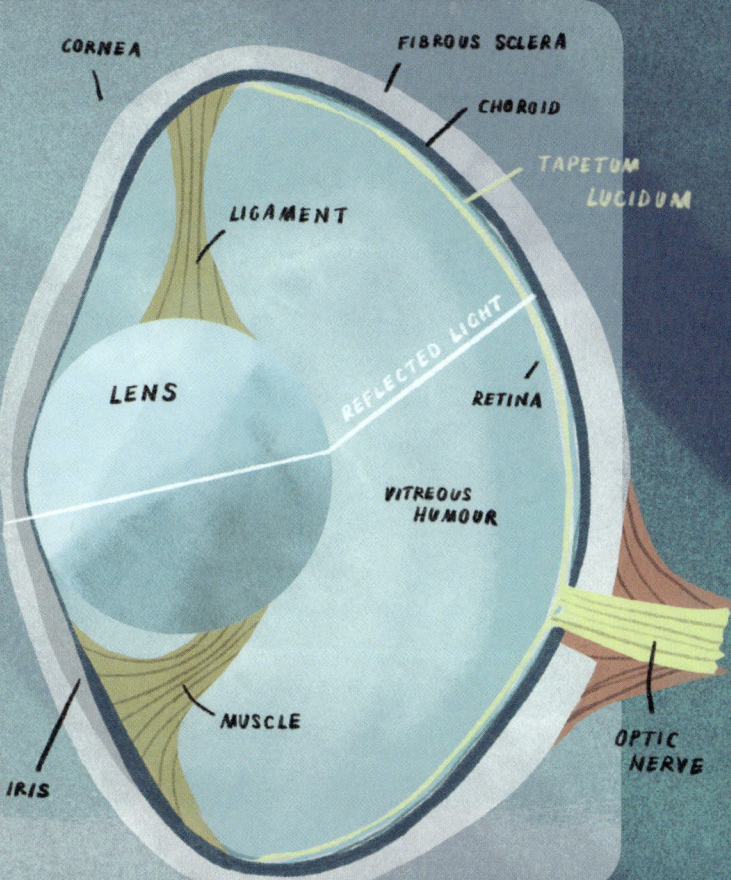

CORNEA
FIBROUS SCLERA
CHOROID
TAPETUM LUCIDUM
LIGAMENT
REFLECTED LIGHT
RETINA
LENS
VITREOUS HUMOUR
MUSCLE
IRIS
OPTIC NERVE

A nurse shark's brilliant barbels

Lip-smacking barbels

Alongside carp, catfish and turtles, some species of shark have barbels. These are small, fleshy flaps near the mouth that contain taste buds and are designed with hunting in mind. If sand or silt get in the way and a shark's eyes aren't up to the job, barbels usually help them root out their next meal. The word means 'little beard', but they can also grow from the chin or nostrils.

FAST⚡FACT

Nobody's sure why they're called nurse sharks, but historians think their sucking mouths may have reminded sailors of nursing infants.

CHOMP

Practice makes perfect when it comes to prey-snaring skills. Sharks have spent millions of years honing their hunting methods. Here's a bite-size guide to the many surprising ways they go in for the kill...

Sniff!
Wiggle your hand in a sink full of water... Can you feel the motion it creates? Sharks detect prey in a similar way, by picking up on water movement nearby using a highly sensitive tube, known as the lateral line, that runs down their body.

GREAT WHITES HAVE A SPECIAL SYSTEM THAT KEEPS THEIR MUSCLES WARM AND READY TO CHARGE!

LATERAL LINE

SOME SHARKS PRACTISE HUNTING SKILLS WHEN THEY'RE TEENAGERS

Invisible signals
A smattering of small pores over a shark's snout are on high alert for wave-like electrical impulses sent out by other creatures.

Stalkers!
Some seabed-dwelling shark species use camouflage to sneak up on their next unsuspecting meal. Splotched, patterned backs allow them to blend in seamlessly with the reef, while the angelshark even has a flattened body shape to melt into the sand of the ocean floor.

CAN YOU SPOT IT?

Masters of disguise
Most sharks are shades of black or brown on top and have pale undersides. Seen from above, their dark backs blend into deep water. Seen from below, their bellies blend with the pale sky. Clever, heh?

1 THE BUMP AND BITE

SPECIES
Bull shark, great white

HOW? The shark positions itself below a sea lion or seal, before torpedoing upwards at full speed. It hits its target, mouth wide open, before biting down to kill it instantly. The shark's unique feeding technique sees the razor-sharp teeth on its lower jaw hold onto the carcass while its upper jaw teeth 'saw' backwards and forwards. It's a bit like the way you use your knife and fork – but a lot messier!

2 SPYHOPPING AND BREACHING

SPECIES
Whitehop, great white

HOW? Sharks pop their heads above the surface to get a closer look at their prey by keeping their body almost vertical! They then sink back into the depths before shooting up to breach, which stuns their prey as it's tossed high in the air.

3 THE CRUSH AND WHIP

SPECIES
Hammerhead, thresher

HOW? The strange-looking hammerhead has the smallest mouth of any shark species, but uses its wide head to pin stingrays to the ocean floor before chowing down. The thresher shark has the longest tail of any species and unleashes it to whip and stun prey. Threshers also use it to gather up shoals of smaller fish into their waiting jaws!

MANY SHARKS ARE PRECOCIAL. THIS MEANS THEY'RE READY TO HUNT PREY **STRAIGHT AFTER BIRTH!**

#Teamshark

Sevengill sharks buck the trend for the typical shark habit of **SOLO HUNTING**. They round up their friends to capture the fur seal, which is too large for them to overpower on their own.

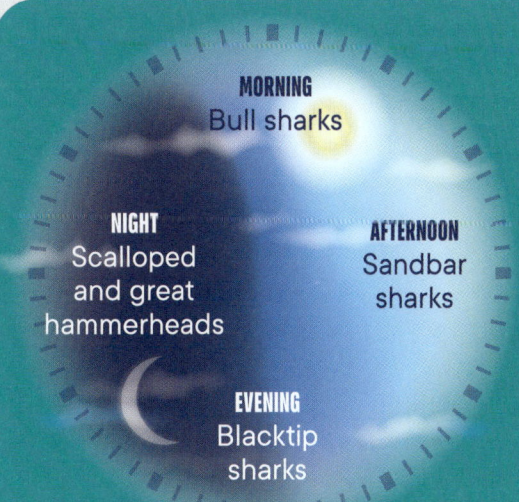

MORNING
Bull sharks

NIGHT
Scalloped and great hammerheads

AFTERNOON
Sandbar sharks

EVENING
Blacktip sharks

Shift pattern
Shark species favour different times of day for hunting! It's thought they cunningly adapted to avoid bumping into each other at mealtimes and take turns in sharing the bounty.

DINNER TIME!

This feast of shark facts puts these predators' eating habits into perspective... Tuck in and you might find a few surprises!

Most shark species are meat-eaters (carnivores), so they eat creatures that are below them in the food chain, such as seals, octopus, mackerel, crabs and lobster. But three species – basking sharks, whale sharks and megamouth sharks – are planktivores, which means they're content to feast on marine plankton (plants) and zooplankton (teeny tiny living organisms).

Plankton are marine drifters carried along by tides and currents

EATS THESE TINY PLANKTON

SOME SPECIES OF SHARK CAN GO THREE MONTHS WITHOUT A SCRAP TO EAT!

Great white shark swimming and hunting

Great white diet

One third of a great white shark's menu is made up of pelagic (mid-ocean swimming) fish such as salmon. Open wide and say 'pel-AH-jic'!

The great white can make a 30kg meal (which is less than 3% of its body weight) last around six weeks at a time. Humans eat around 2% of our body weight every day, while sharks only eat every two to three days. So sharks really aren't that greedy!

Leave some for me!

Sharks like to dine solo, but if any others sense fresh grub is up for grabs they rush to get in on the action – snapping wildly at each other at the same time.

Blacktip reef sharks fighting for a bite

I'LL EAT ANYTHING... I'M NOT FUSSY!

Tiger sharks are nicknamed 'rubbish bins of the sea' because they're not picky eaters. From sea turtles to snakes and even other sharks, they'll scoff them all! Carrion (the decaying flesh of dead animals) is also a favourite snack.

STRANGE BUT TRUE!

Some very odd things have been found inside shark stomachs

Chicken coop
It's a mystery how a complete cage, complete with chickens, found its way into the ocean in the first place. Could a twister have whisked it up? Do you have a better theory?

A suit of armour (and skeleton!)
Did the 16th-century knight wearing a suit of armour decide to challenge a great white shark to a duel to the death? Either way, he lost!

Tyres
About one million tyres were dumped in the ocean around 50 years ago to create a man-made reef. It didn't work, so sharks gobbled them up instead.

Tom-tom drums
A tiger shark in Senegal was certainly dancing to the beat of its own drum when it swallowed a set of these!

Polar bear
Polar bears can weigh up to 500kg (roughly 15 average-sized 10-year-olds!) so the Arctic-dwelling green shark that ate it must've been seriously hungry...

SPIT ME OUT AT ONCE, I SAY! I YIELD!

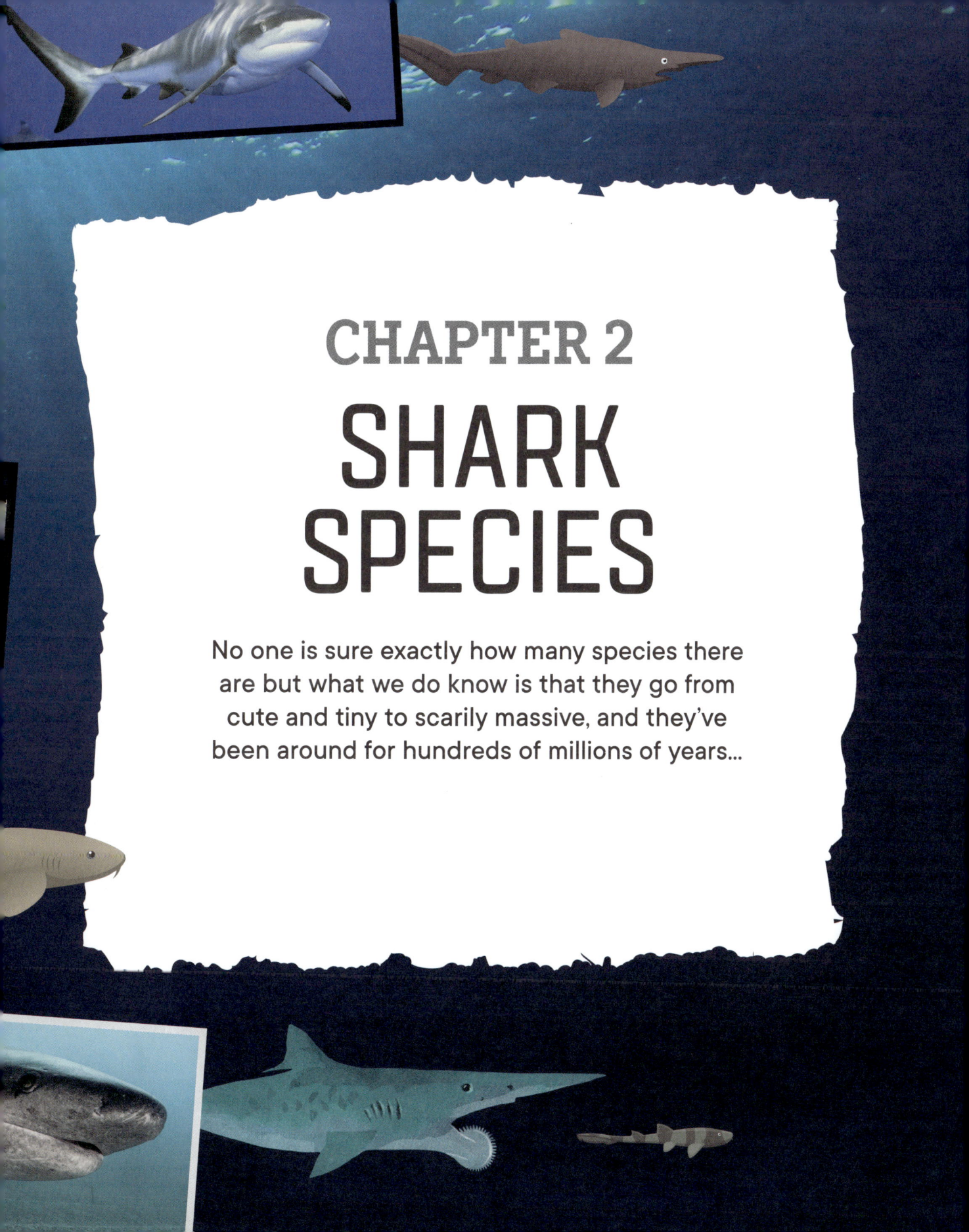

CHAPTER 2

SHARK SPECIES

No one is sure exactly how many species there are but what we do know is that they go from cute and tiny to scarily massive, and they've been around for hundreds of millions of years...

SIZING UP SHARKS

OCEANIC WHITETIP SHARK 4M

Sharks range in size from the biggest fish on the planet to the size of your palm!

COOKIECUTTER SHARK 0.42M

THRESHER SHARK 3.3M

↑ LONGNOSE SAWSHARK 1.4M

↑ WHALE SHARK 12M

↑ GREAT WHITE SHARK 6M

↑ FRILLED SHARK 1.6M

34

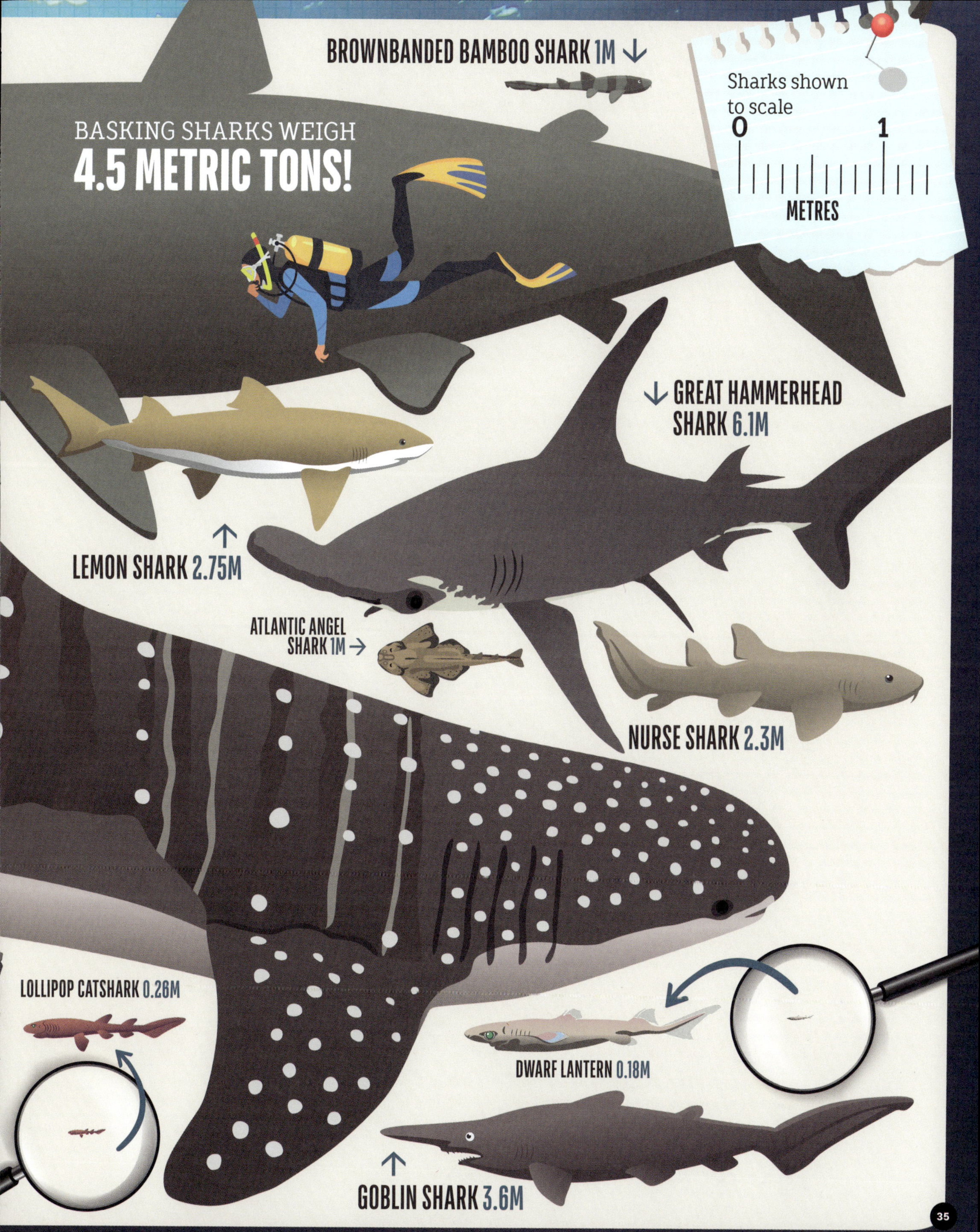

BROWNBANDED BAMBOO SHARK 1M
Sharks shown to scale
0 1
METRES
BASKING SHARKS WEIGH
4.5 METRIC TONS!
GREAT HAMMERHEAD SHARK 6.1M
LEMON SHARK 2.75M
ATLANTIC ANGEL SHARK 1M
NURSE SHARK 2.3M
LOLLIPOP CATSHARK 0.28M
DWARF LANTERN 0.18M
GOBLIN SHARK 3.6M

PREHISTORIC PREDATORS

It's no wonder sharks rule the waves today – their ancestors were sharpening their hunting skills hundreds of millions of years ago. Long since extinct, these predators were deadly in their heyday!

BUZZSAW SHARK →

You must be next-level tough if you made it through a mass-level extinction when 95% of species didn't. The Helicoprion, also known as the buzzsaw shark thanks to a famously spiralling set of teeth, survived the Great Permian extinction 250 million years ago. Although it would eventually become extinct 25 million years later, scientists think the Helicoprion was the first shark to regrow rows of teeth. No wonder – its underbite needed hundreds!

FIRST SHARK TO REGROW TEETH?

SCISSOR-TOOTHED SHARK ↙

Think a shark's jaws are only useful for chomping down? How about swordfighting? The Edestus might look like it's puckering up for a kiss, but this scissor-toothed savage used the strangely shaped whorl in its mouth to slice prey as it thrashed around. It's the only creature ever known to use this hunting technique. It worked for a while, as the species thrived for 20 million years before becoming extinct 300 million years ago.

FACT UNLIKE MOST SHARKS, THE EDESTUS DID NOT SHED ITS **SCISSOR TEETH** WHEN THEY WORE DOWN. INSTEAD THEY **GREW CONTINUOUSLY** THROUGHOUT ITS LIFE.

SPINY SHARK ↘

The Acanthodian, also known as the spiny shark, belonged to an extinct class of gnathostomes (or 'jawed fish'). It was one of the first ever animals to have a hinged jaw and is an example of a 'transitional species' – somewhere between a fish and a shark. It had a bendy cartilage skeleton like a modern shark, but its fins were lined with tiny, bony spines similar to the ray-finned fish we see today. It seems as though bony fish muscled in on this shark's space in the food chain!

ANVIL SHARK ↘

The Stethacanthus was a smaller shark-like fish that has been extinct for around 300 million years. While it had a version of the vertical dorsal fin we know today, the anvil shark is famous for its antennae-like backpiece with an armour-plated flat top. How do we know what it looked like? The 'Bearsden Shark' fossil, found in Scotland, belongs to an anvil shark and is one of the most complete cartilage skeletons ever discovered!

FACT THE ANVIL SHARK ALSO HAD STUNNING **PECTORAL FIN WHIPS** – FINE, VINE-LIKE FINS THAT LIKELY LASHED OUT TO MAKE LIGHT WORK OF SMALLER PREY!

WHICH SHARK ON THIS PAGE HAD
490 RAZOR-SHARP TEETH?

GINSU SHARK ←

Have you ever wondered exactly when the shark became the ocean's No 1 predator? Well, the Cretoxyrhina (or Ginsu shark) ruled the waves around 100 to 75 million years ago. The Ginsu would eat anything – from dinosaurs like the Pteranodon to the world's largest-ever turtle, the Archelon. 'Ginsu' is a brand of extremely sharp knives, so it's no wonder the Cretoxyrhina got this nickname – it had up to 490 razor-sharp 7cm teeth!

EEL SHARK ↘

Think the Xenacanthus looks like a unicorn? Look closer at its gormless expression and sharp teeth and you'll see why it's better known as the eel shark. There's a striking resemblance to the modern-day moray eel, which is no surprise considering how much they have in common! This ancient freshwater shark, with its pretty, ribbon-like fin, grew to 1m in length and died out about 202 million years ago.

FACT THE EEL SHARK WAS WELL PROTECTED THANKS TO THE **SHARP SPINE** PROTRUDING FROM ITS NECK, JUST LIKE A STINGRAY'S **VENOMOUS BARB**.

...and, of course, the famous
MEGALODON THE BIGGEST EVER SHARK

TURN OVER to learn about this ancient beast!

MEET THE MEG!

Possibly the biggest (and definitely the most terrifying) fish ever to have evolved, 20 million years ago the megalodon – aka the Megatooth – was so massive it ate whales for breakfast. Time to hide!

Mega monster

Scientists think these prehistoric predators weighed in at a whopping 50–75 tons, which is heavy enough to make even the toughest sailor's heart sink. Megalodons were the largest sharks and among the biggest fish ever to have existed. How do we know this when no skeletons have been found? Well, only a beast this big would leave behind terrifying teeth fossils up to 18cm in length!

18cm LONG

Megalodon teeth have been found on every continent apart from Antarctica.

Big mouth, big problems

Dolphins, humpback whales, sea lions and even other large sharks were all on the megalodon's menu. No wonder – it's estimated that the Meg's jaw was a gobsmacking 2.7 metres tall and 3.4 metres wide. That's big enough to swallow two adult humans in one big bite! But a big body meant the Meg needed 1,100kg of food every day and scientists reckon this ferocious appetite was one of its downfalls.

UH-OH!

Still out there somewhere?

Could the Meg still be lurking in the depths? It's highly unlikely. This huge hunter couldn't adapt to its changing environment. Unlike humans, animals have a harder time moving to a new place to find food. Legend has it they migrated towards the mysterious Mariana Trench in the Pacific. But the chilly abyss of the world's deepest ocean point wouldn't have suited these warm-water sharks.

THE MEG WENT EXTINCT AROUND
3.6 MILLION
YEARS AGO

Not quite great white

Most CGI reconstructions of the Meg make it look just like a giant great white shark, but this might not be the case! With a fearsome family tree that stretches back all the way to the Cretaceous period (145–66 million years ago), the two species aren't quite as closely linked as once thought. The Meg likely had a flatter face, a squidged-in snout and extra-long pectoral fins to support its truly mammoth size and weight.

The whole tooth

Megalodons had serrated multi-layered teeth and they could make their way through as many as 40,000 of them in their 20-40 years hunting the ocean's murky depths.

Because most of the Meg's carcass was made from cartilage not bone, almost all that remains of the beast are its fossilised teeth. Fragments of these signature gnashers have even been found embedded in whale bones. The Meg's full name is Otodus megalodon, which means 'big, ear-shaped tooth'.

3.4 metres wide

2.7 metres tall

40,000 TEETH IN ITS LIFETIME

SOME MEGS WERE 18M. THAT'S ALMOST AS LONG AS A CRICKET PITCH!

MARVELS OF
THE DEEP

Their prehistoric playmates may no longer roam the ocean, but many sharks of a similar vintage still do! Meet some of the oldest-surviving species swimming today

BROADNOSE SEVENGILL SHARK

The broadnose sevengill is, simply put, more primitive than most modern sharks. Fossils from the Jurassic Period (200 to 145 million years ago) show ancient sharks with seven gills, instead of the usual five, so they've been around a long time. They might not look like typical sharks, but they're powerful hunters. Broadnose sevengill sharks can grow up to 2.2m and have a legendary appetite – they've been known to feed on everything from crustaceans to seals. They're not picky!

500 YEARS OLD?

I BET YOU'D MOVE SLOWLY TOO IF YOU WERE 500!

GREENLAND SHARK ↑

The world's longest-living vertebrate (a creature with a backbone) likes to take things slow! Greenland sharks can live for up to 500 years – that's five times longer than the giant tortoise and twice as long as the United States has been a country! They're a tricky species to study, as they dwell in the deepest, coldest waters of the Arctic and North Atlantic ocean, but scientists have revealed that these 6m-long sharks aren't ready to start having pups until they're 150 years old!

NOT PICKY WILL EAT ANYTHING!

SNEAKY SEABIRD EATER

FRILLED SHARK ↓

Frilled sharks have changed remarkably little in 80 million years. They're considered cousins of great whites and hammerhead sharks, but we don't see the resemblance! The frills they're named for refer to their six pairs of fringed gills and their 300 needlepoint teeth snap shut like a deadly snare, meaning these 2m-long terrors can swallow prey half their size whole.

ANGELSHARK ↑

It might look like a ray, but the angelshark is a member of the squatinidae group – they're one big flat family! Angelsharks have been around for 150 million years but are now threatened by fishing practices. They're incredible hunters themselves, though, using their pectoral fins to bury themselves beneath the sand in Mediterranean and northeast Atlantic waters. Angelsharks are so effective, they've been known to snack on seabirds!

300 TEETH

FACT JUST LIKE THE RINGS ON A TREE, MANY SHARKS CAN BE AGED BY COUNTING THE **GROWTH BANDS ON THEIR SPINE**'S CONNECTING VERTEBRAE.

CAVE LURKER

TASSELLED WOBBEGONG ←

This is one carpet you don't want to step on! Looking more like something from *Star Wars* than a shark, the tasselled wobbegong first evolved its distinct features 11 million years ago. This 2m-long living bear trap hides in the coral reefs of Australia and New Guinea and flattens out to blend in with its surroundings. The wobbegong sticks to night missions so it's even harder to spot and gobbles prey half its size. Lurking in caves, it lures smaller fish in before blocking the exit!

ORDER *of the* OCEAN

Sharks are one big family but nobody knows for sure how many species of shark there are. Scientists sort the ones we do know about into orders (or types), based on body features.

CARCHARHINIFORMES

Ground sharks

With close to 300 species, ground sharks have a special membrane protecting their eyes, plus two dorsal fins, anal fins and five gill slits.

CATSHARK

HETERODONTIFORMES

Bullhead sharks

The bullhead family has nine known species, and they're 1.65m or shorter. They're tropical and subtropical bottom-feeders.

ZEBRA BULLHEAD SHARK

HEXANCHIFORMES

Cow sharks

With just seven surviving species, Hexanchiformes are the most primitive group of sharks around. They only have one dorsal fin and either six or seven gill slits.

COW SHARK

LAMNIFORMES

Mackerel sharks

With around 20 species, the mackerel shark order includes the great white and is known for having two dorsal fins, an anal fin, five gill slits and eyes lacking a protective membrane.

GREAT WHITE SHARK

ORECTOLOBIFORMES

Carpet sharks
Called carpet sharks because of their beautiful patterns, around 40 species share two spineless dorsal fins, five gill slits and a small mouth that doesn't reach past the eyes.

BLIND SHARK

PRISTIOPHORIFORMES

Sawsharks
With a very long and spiky rostrum (snout or bill) edged with sharp teeth, the eight live species of sawshark use their nose to slash at would-be attackers.

SAWSHARK

SQUALIFORMES

Gulper sharks, kitefin sharks, bramble sharks, lantern sharks, rough sharks, sleeper sharks
There are around 130 species in this group, and they all have two (usually spiny!) dorsal fins, sharp, angled heads and five to seven gill slits to breathe through.

ROUGH SHARK

SQUATINIFORMES

Angelsharks
There are more than 20 species of angelshark, and most of them are classified as critically endangered. These fantastic flat fish have broad pectoral fins that make them look like rays.

ANGELSHARK

MORE SHARKS THIS WAY

ICONS *of the* OCEAN

There's more than 500 species of shark swimming in the sea, and it can be hard to keep track of them! Get to know some of the most iconic sharks in the ocean

SPINY DOGFISH

Also known as the spurdog, the spiny dogfish is the most common shark in the world. It's most likely to be found in the North Atlantic and Pacific oceans.

25221. Neg Em 34455

BONNETHEAD SHARK

The only hammerhead sharks that use their pectoral fins to swim, the bonnethead (or shovelhead) can be found in the North Atlantic ocean and Gulf of Mexico.

FASTER THAN USAIN BOLT?

GREY REEF SHARK

A native of the Indian and Pacific oceans, the grey reef can swim up to 40km/h – that's almost as fast as Usain Bolt, who's clocked 43.99km/h!

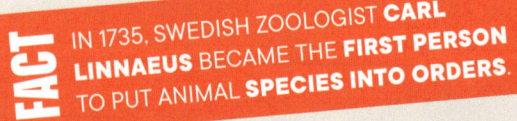

FACT IN 1735, SWEDISH ZOOLOGIST **CARL LINNAEUS** BECAME THE **FIRST PERSON** TO PUT ANIMAL **SPECIES INTO ORDERS**.

COMMON THRESHER SHARK

The largest species of the thresher family is a long-finned legend! It can be found in tropical waters, but the common thresher actually prefers it cooler.

DUSKY SHARK

Found in warmer waters around the world, the dusky shark has been recorded at depths of 400m and will eat just about anything to survive – even starfish!

NURSE SHARK

Found across the globe, the nurse shark is an important species for research because it's so robust and is known to tolerate tagging. It's slow, but it can nip!

ONE OF THE GENTLEST SHARKS

ZEBRA SHARK

Wriggling into narrow nooks and crevices in search of food, the zebra shark uses its striking markings to keep out of harm's way.

PROFILE ON PAGE 50!

GREAT HAMMERHEAD SHARK

They really are great! The largest of all hammerhead species, these square-faced sharks can be 6.1m long! They're solo swimmers and can live more than 40 years.

SHORTFIN MAKO SHARKS

These sharp-looking sharks might be the fastest shark in the sea! They zoom around the Atlantic, Indian and Pacific oceans.

HORN SHARK

Best known for their incredible spiral-shaped egg cases and horny eye ridges, this bullhead shark is found just off America's sunny west coast.

SAND TIGER SHARK

You can find sand tiger sharks swimming along sandy shorelines all over the planet. It might look angry, but this slow-moving species is pretty laidback.

THE GREATEST

Naturally curious and nowhere near as deadly as you may have heard (at least not to humans), the great white gets a bad rep! But there's so much more to these warm -blooded wonders beneath the surface...

Record breacher

The largest predatory fish on earth, the great white shark can sometimes grow up to 6m long. That's as tall as a giraffe! They have a pretty streamlined shape for such huge hunters, backed up by powerful tails that propel them through the ocean at unbelievable speeds. And its tail is so strong, this wild giant can whip itself right out of the sea! This is known as breaching and great whites can clear the water by five metres.

DETECTS 1 DROP OF BLOOD IN 10 BILLION DROPS OF WATER!

GREAT WHITES CAN JUMP 5 METRES CLEAR OF THE WATER

DATA

OTHER NAMES Carcharodon carcharias (from the Greek for 'sharpen teeth')

LENGTH Up to 6m

WEIGHT Up to 2,200kg

LIFESPAN Up to 30 years

SPEED 40km/h

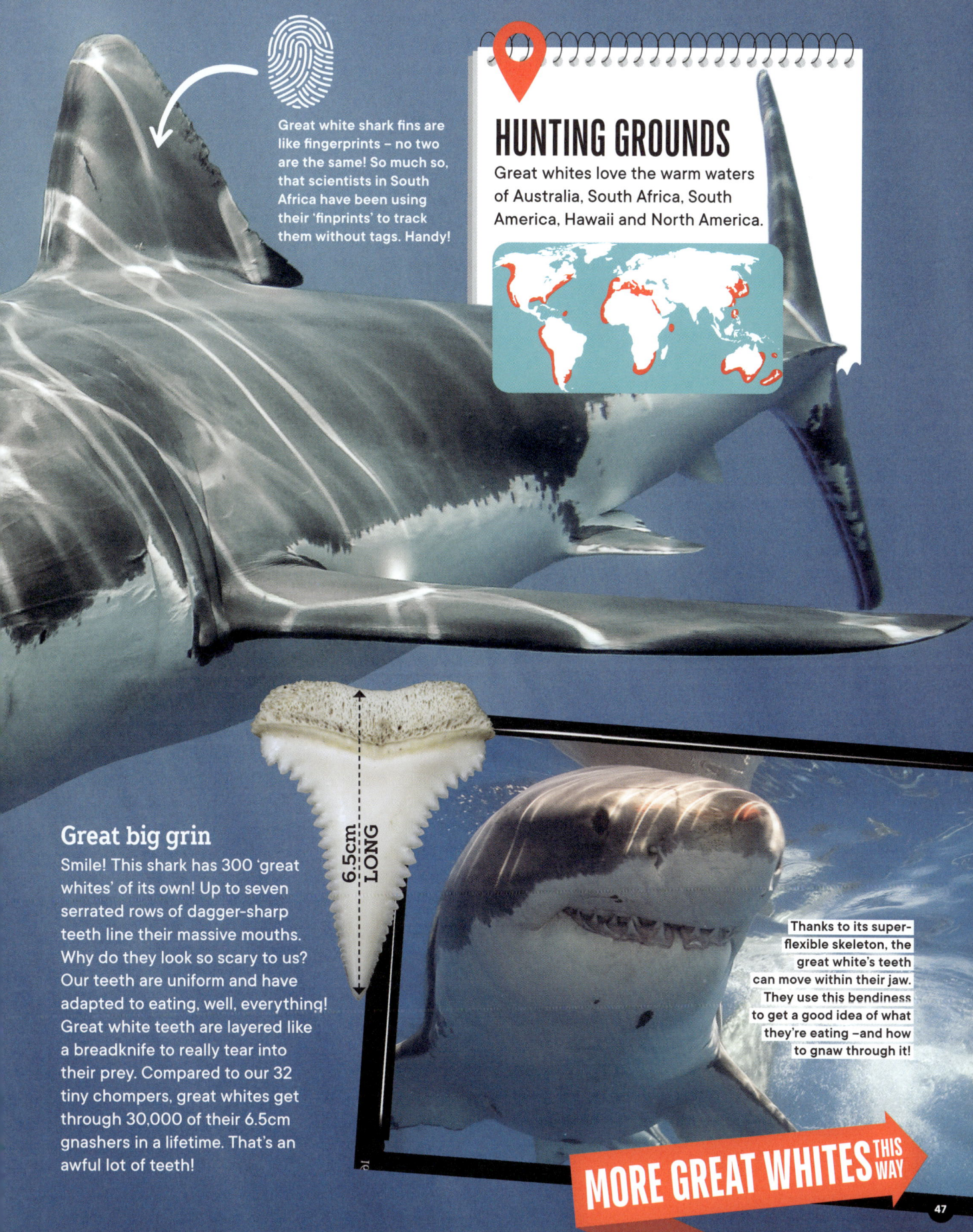

Great white shark fins are like fingerprints – no two are the same! So much so, that scientists in South Africa have been using their 'finprints' to track them without tags. Handy!

HUNTING GROUNDS

Great whites love the warm waters of Australia, South Africa, South America, Hawaii and North America.

Great big grin

Smile! This shark has 300 'great whites' of its own! Up to seven serrated rows of dagger-sharp teeth line their massive mouths. Why do they look so scary to us? Our teeth are uniform and have adapted to eating, well, everything! Great white teeth are layered like a breadknife to really tear into their prey. Compared to our 32 tiny chompers, great whites get through 30,000 of their 6.5cm gnashers in a lifetime. That's an awful lot of teeth!

6.5cm LONG

Thanks to its super-flexible skeleton, the great white's teeth can move within their jaw. They use this bendiness to get a good idea of what they're eating –and how to gnaw through it!

MORE GREAT WHITES THIS WAY

Sneak through the sea

How does such a large shark sneak up on its prey? The great white's colours and camouflage are perfectly suited for the sea. The deeper you get in water, the less you can see, and the great white uses this dimming light to its advantage. From the top, the simple grey-blue skin matches the ocean around it, while the bright bottom side (the ventral side) looks like a patch of sunlight dancing on the water's surface. It can't be seen!

SPOT THE SHARK!

When great whites attack their prey, they **whip their tails** to make their **teeth sink even deeper** into tasty seals!

Massive menu

So, if people are off the menu, then what's a shark to feast on? When they're young pups, great whites will hunt smaller prey like fish and rays. As they grow into adults, they like to chow down on chunky sea lions, seals and whales – any species with enough fat and meat on the bone to make the massive effort of attacking worth it. Humans just aren't packing all the meat they need!

EATS

Big mouth... tiny tongue!

There's a reason nobody talks about shark tongues – they're not that impressive! Hidden in the great white's massive maw is a simple chunk of cartilage called a basihyal. It's short, small, has no taste buds and isn't very flexible, so why is it there? For most species, it sits in place to protect the mouth and gills. Like humans, the great white has taste buds in its mouth and throat, but they're not strong. After all, they're not famous for being fussy eaters!

SHARK ATTACK?

FEWER THAN 5 PEOPLE DIE FROM SHARK ATTACKS EACH YEAR

SHARKS

They're more wary of us than we are of them

Think a great white will gobble you up? It's not likely! Scientists have calculated how likely you are to get snapped by a shark and there's a tiny 1 in 3,748,076 chance! If anything, they should be afraid of us – humans kill 100 million sharks each year due to fishing practices. According to stats from the Florida Museum of Natural History, fewer than five people die from shark bites each year... and that's the tooth!

Safe in the sea

In 1975, the movie *Jaws* changed the way the world saw sharks forever. In the Steven Spielberg film, a great white terrorises a small town. While it's not based on truth, it put 'galeophobia' (a fear of sharks) at the top of many people's list of terrors. Tragically, *Jaws* made sharks seem not just scary, but also more valuable to hunters. Even the original novel's writer Peter Benchley says he regrets making some people think it was unsafe to go back in the water.

GOTTA KEEP MOVIN'

Thankfully, the tide has turned on whether sharks should be kept in captivity – for great whites, it comes down to their breathing. Because their gills work by funnelling water through their mouths as they move, there simply isn't enough space or oxygen for great whites when they're kept in captivity. Small blood vessels in their gills suck up the oxygen in the ocean in a process called obligate ram ventilation..

'Knowing what I know now, I could never write that book today. Sharks don't target human beings, and they certainly don't hold grudges!'
Peter Benchley

JAWS

HAMMER TIME!

Of all the eye-catching fish in the ocean, the great hammerhead shark really stands out, thanks to its distinctive shadow. But this quirky-looking character does a lot more than just look cool...

ENDANGERED

Young wonders

Hammerheads have been around for 23 million years, which sounds like a long time, right? Wrong! Compared with cow, frilled and goblin sharks, they're the *new fish on the block!* It's thought that evolving in a modern habitat gave hammerheads the same survival skills as older species, alongside a suite of their own superpowers. They have slow growth rates and wide eyes that keep them out of harm's way – plus they give birth to live pups.

THESE GUYS HAVE ONLY BEEN AROUND 2 MILLION YEARS! AND THEY CALL ME THE YOUNG ONE?!

DATA

LENGTH Up to 6.1m

WEIGHT 230-450kg

TOP SPEED 40km/h

LIFESPAN 20-40 years

CONSERVATION STATUS Endangered

Seeing things differently

Having binocular vision (that is, two eyes) grants thousands of species the useful ability to sense how far away things really are. Well, imagine if your head was 1.5m wide with big, bulgy eyes! It gives the great hammerhead an incredible, all-round field of view of 360°, but it can't see right in front of its own face! Thankfully it doesn't need to, because its cephalofoils (head stalks) are covered in electrosensitive organs that help it hunt through silt on the seabed and gobble up bottom-feeders.

HAMMERHEAD HOTSPOTS 📍

The great hammerhead shark likes to travel and can be found all over the world, particularly off the coast of South America, West Africa and southeast Asia. While preferring mild and tropical waters, coral reefs, continental shelves and lagoons, this fish isn't fussy about how deep the sea is. It can be found near the shore in water as shallow

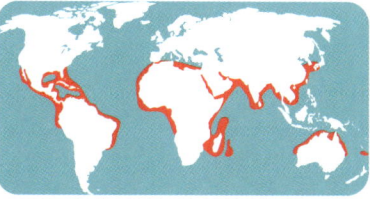

as 1m or far out at depths of 80m. Unusually for sharks, some hammerhead species swim in large groups (known as 'shivers') of 100 or more. But the great hammerhead prefers its own company, hunting alone and migrating long distances of up to 1,200km all by itself.

Scalloped hammerhead shark

Meet the family

One of 10 species, the great hammerhead has 'cousins' who come in various shapes, colours and sizes – but all share that same-shaped bonce. Others have cool-sounding names – there are scalloped, smooth, smalleye and whitefin hammerheads. Winghead, bonnethead and scoophead sharks are also part of the family. And there's even the scalloped bonnethead! The most recent addition, the Carolina hammerhead, was officially recognised in 2013. That's a lot of hammers!

YUM!

Hunting skills

The great hammerhead is a carnivore (meat-eater) with long, serrated teeth that look like small triangular saw blades. These are perfect for tucking into prey such as octopus, squid, jellyfish and even hard-shelled crustaceans such as lobsters. That mallet-shaped head also comes in handy for pinning down those slippery stingrays against the sea floor as the shark feeds on their fins. In fact, its head is so wide that it acts like wings on an aeroplane to give it a 'lift' while swimming and make tight turns. Just another amazing example of the species' ability to perfectly adapt to its environment.

SAVE OUR SHARKS

Like all sharks, the great hammerhead is an apex predator, which means it has few – if any – natural enemies. Even so, it's now an endangered species. Why? It's been fished heavily for its large dorsal fin, which is considered a delicacy in many countries (especially in Asia).

GRACEFUL GIANTS

When is a whale not a whale? When it's a whale shark! And that's just the first surprise this majestic marine creature has up its fins...

Spotted off the coast

Whale sharks are grey, blue or brown on top with a white belly, and each one has its own unique pattern of pale-yellow spots across its back. This speckled motif allows individual whales to be identified in much the same way fingerprints help pinpoint humans. Another feature that makes this fish stand out is its mouth, which is positioned bizarrely on the side of its head and measures 1.5m in width!

DATA

SIZE 12m

WEIGHT 19,000kg

AVERAGE SPEED 5km/h

LIFESPAN 80-130

CONSERVATION STATUS Endangered

THE **LARGEST WHALE SHARK** EVER RECORDED WAS **18.8M LONG**

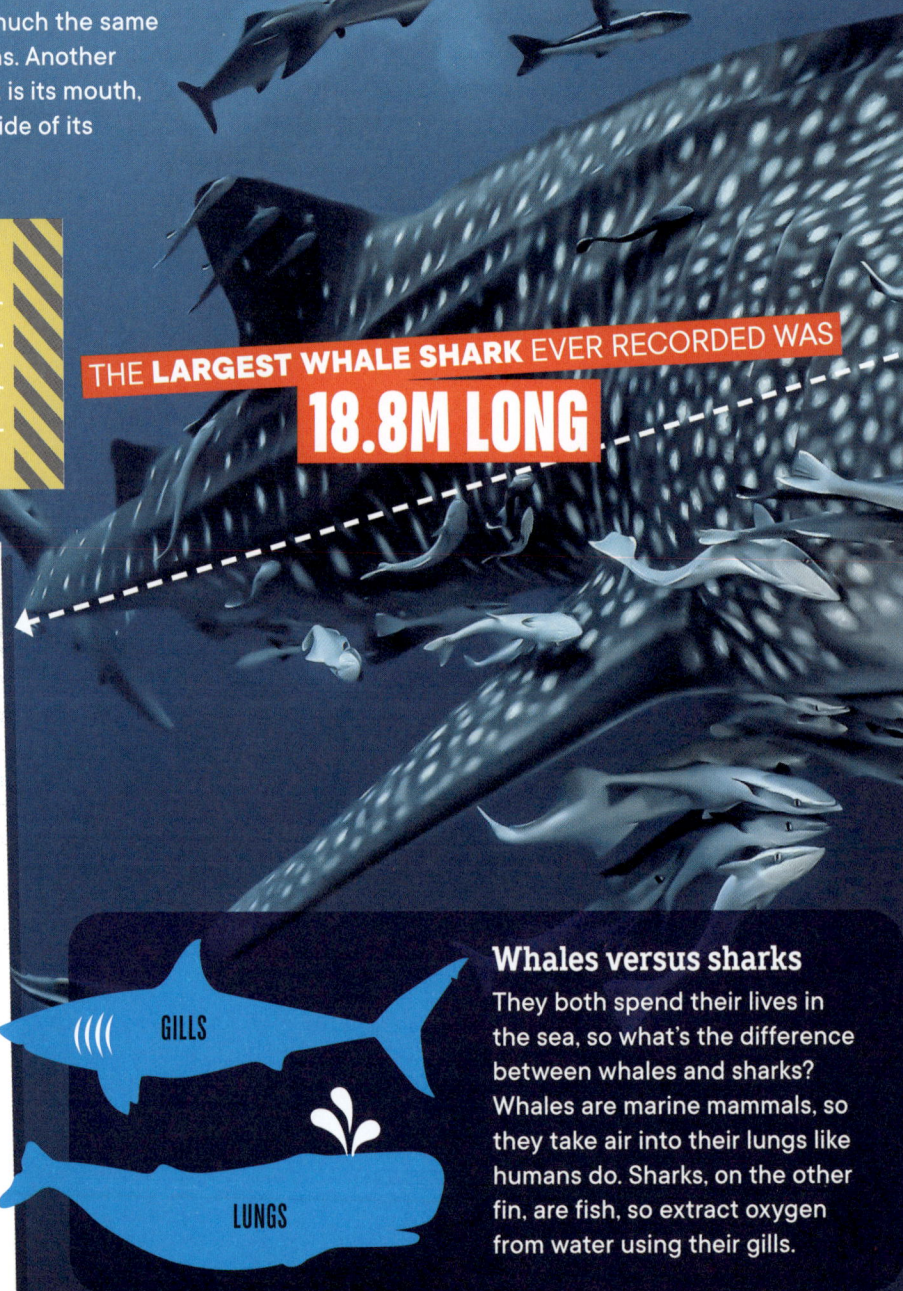

Big fish

Despite its mammalian namesake, the whale shark is not a marine mammal – it's a fish. But it's the biggest fish in the world, measuring an average of 12m long and weighing around 19,000kg – that's roughly the length and weight of a double-decker bus! Happily for humans, whale sharks are often referred to as 'gentle giants' and will even let swimmers hitch a ride. But don't expect to be whooshed through the waves because this graceful beast prefers a slower pace of life compared with most sharks – it cruises along at only 5km/h. Calm seas ahead!

GILLS

LUNGS

Whales versus sharks

They both spend their lives in the sea, so what's the difference between whales and sharks? Whales are marine mammals, so they take air into their lungs like humans do. Sharks, on the other fin, are fish, so extract oxygen from water using their gills.

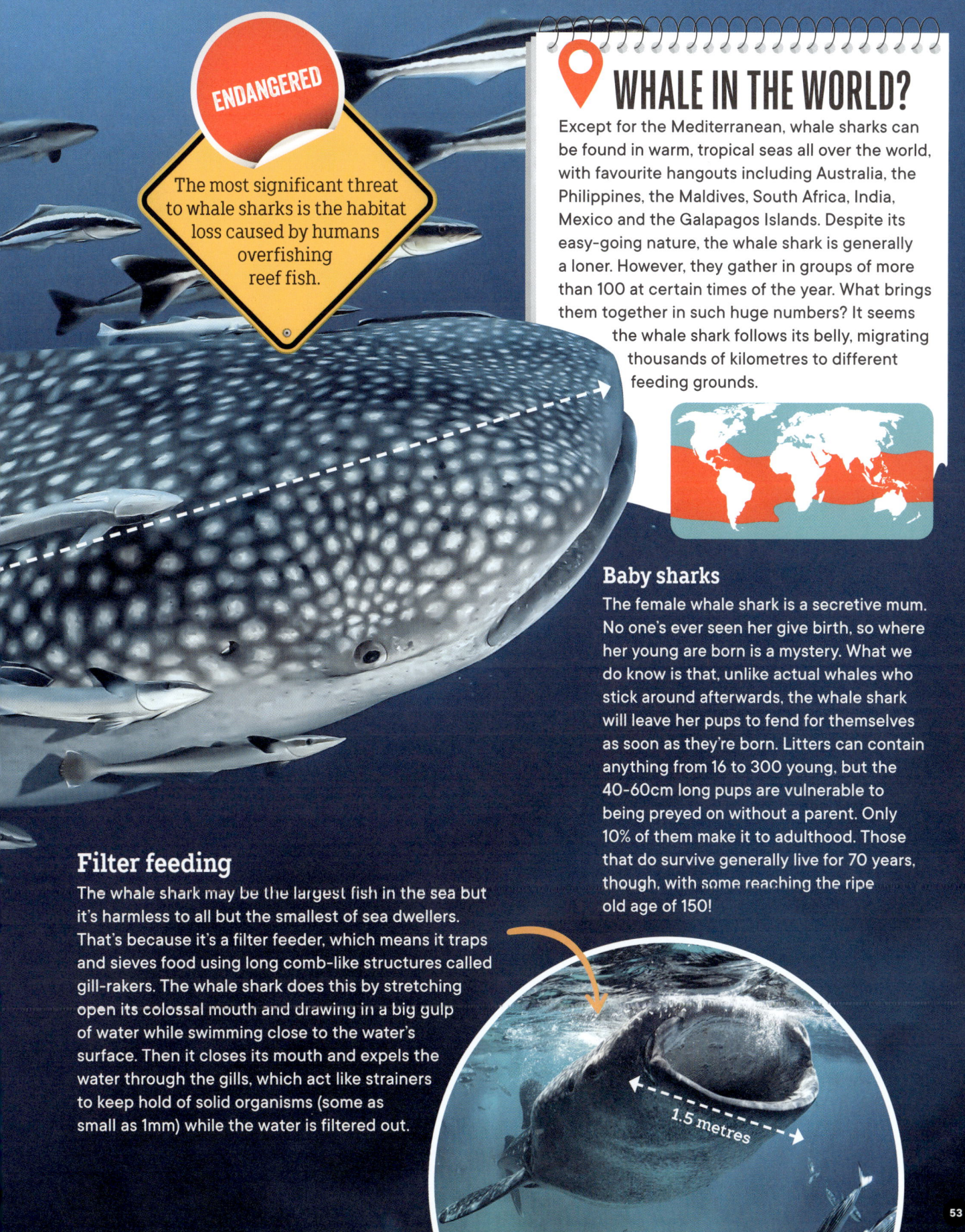

The most significant threat to whale sharks is the habitat loss caused by humans overfishing reef fish.

WHALE IN THE WORLD?

Except for the Mediterranean, whale sharks can be found in warm, tropical seas all over the world, with favourite hangouts including Australia, the Philippines, the Maldives, South Africa, India, Mexico and the Galapagos Islands. Despite its easy-going nature, the whale shark is generally a loner. However, they gather in groups of more than 100 at certain times of the year. What brings them together in such huge numbers? It seems the whale shark follows its belly, migrating thousands of kilometres to different feeding grounds.

Baby sharks

The female whale shark is a secretive mum. No one's ever seen her give birth, so where her young are born is a mystery. What we do know is that, unlike actual whales who stick around afterwards, the whale shark will leave her pups to fend for themselves as soon as they're born. Litters can contain anything from 16 to 300 young, but the 40-60cm long pups are vulnerable to being preyed on without a parent. Only 10% of them make it to adulthood. Those that do survive generally live for 70 years, though, with some reaching the ripe old age of 150!

Filter feeding

The whale shark may be the largest fish in the sea but it's harmless to all but the smallest of sea dwellers. That's because it's a filter feeder, which means it traps and sieves food using long comb-like structures called gill-rakers. The whale shark does this by stretching open its colossal mouth and drawing in a big gulp of water while swimming close to the water's surface. Then it closes its mouth and expels the water through the gills, which act like strainers to keep hold of solid organisms (some as small as 1mm) while the water is filtered out.

1.5 metres

TIGERS *of the* SEA

The tiger shark has a ferocious reputation, so it might come as a surprise to learn this feisty fish has earned its stripes as an eco-warrior

NEAR THREATENED

TWICE AS HEAVY AS A HIPPO

Easy tiger?

With black stripes running along its streamlined body, there's no mystery behind the tiger shark's name. And just like the big cat on land, this big fish is a fearsome predator. Reaching lengths of 4.25m and a maximum mass of 900kg (heavier than two hippopotamuses), the tiger shark is considered a danger to almost every living creature in the sea – including humans. Despite its aggressive nature, attacks on humans are extremely rare and, when they do happen, tend to be accidental run-ins. This is down to the fact that tiger sharks will try a bite of just about anything, including driftwood and bits of metal. Want to find out more about this misunderstood fish? Swim this way…

DATA

SIZE 3.25-4.25m

WEIGHT Up to 900kg

TOP SPEED 32km/h

LIFESPAN 20-50 years

CONSERVATION STATUS Near threatened

TIGER TRAIL

Tiger sharks are most at home in tropical to warm temperate waters all over the world, including the Americas, the Gulf of Mexico and the Caribbean Sea. While this fish enjoys the coastal life in waters as shallow as 3m, it can also be been seen way out in oceans as deep as 350m. Like most sharks, the tiger doesn't call just one place home, preferring to travel around as it chases the warmer currents.

Go-faster stripes

Against the tiger shark's blueish-green to brown skin and pale belly, its famous stripes don't just look cool – they also provide it with a nifty camouflage that resembles an underwater shadow. The babies are born with dark spots that eventually join together to form the tiger stripes, which then slowly fade as the shark gets older. With a long tail that provides quick bursts of speed, a high back and a dorsal fin that acts as a pivot, the tiger shark is one super-nimble fish!

KILLER INSTINCT

The second-largest predatory shark after the great white, the tiger shark comes with a mouthful of razor-sharp teeth. If you could open up the jaws of this fish (something we don't advise trying!), you'd see that each tooth is serrated around the edges and has tips that point sideways. Not only do these teeth help the shark hold on to wriggly prey – they're also perfect for cutting through thick skin and hard bones.

THE ECO-WARRIOR

We all know how important the rainforests are for the health of our planet, but did you know that seagrass meadows store twice as much CO_2 per square kilometre as on-land forests do? Manatees love munching on seagrass, eating up to 90kg every day. That's why it's important that tiger sharks – natural predators of these huge herbivores – keep the manatee population in check. They're helping to protect the ecosystem.

FRESHWATER WONDERS

Most sharks live in saltwater environments, such as seas, oceans, and coastal areas. But a few species – known as freshwater sharks – have adapted to live in rivers and lakes

There are around 40 species of shark that sometimes swim through fresh water searching for prey. But it's thought that very few can live in this kind of water for long periods of time. This is because sharks need salt in their bodies to survive. Their bodies are designed to match the seawater around them, so contain a lot of salt. Sharks use a process called osmoregulation to maintain the balance of salt and water in their bodies, taking in water to make sure the salinity (amount of salt) in their body matches the surrounding water.

Fresh water has barely any salinity, so most sharks find it hard to balance the salt and water in their bodies when they're in such a non-salty environment. Swimming in fresh water dehydrates most sharks, dulls their senses and can even make them sink!

However, freshwater sharks are fine because they're able to adjust their salt and water ratios and can recycle the salt in their bodies. They also have less dense livers, which tends to make them more buoyant. So clever!

SPEARTOOTH SHARK ↗

These sturdy sharks are able to handle different salinity levels, so they can swim both in saltwater and freshwater environments. Native to New Guinea and northern Australia, speartooth sharks grow to 3m long and usually live in fast-flowing estuaries and rivers. With their wide heads, flattened snouts and small eyes, they preserve energy by using water currents to carry themselves upstream as they hunt for fish, stingrays and crustaceans on the riverbed.

FACT **BULL SHARKS** CAN SWIM THOUSANDS OF KILOMETRES UPRIVER. THEY'VE BEEN SPOTTED IN AMERICA'S MISSISSIPPI RIVER **MORE THAN 2,700KM** AWAY FROM THE OCEAN.

BORNEO RIVER SHARK ↘

One of the worlds' rarest freshwater sharks, the Borneo river shark is only found in the Kinabatangan River. This slate-grey shark grows up to 78cm long and feeds on bony fish such as sardines and tuna.

KINABATANGAN RIVER, BORNEO

NORTHERN RIVER SHARK ↙

The largest species of freshwater shark – at 3m long – is the Northern River shark, which lives in the tidal rivers, estuaries and bays of Northern Australia and New Guinea. These sharks have grey-blue and white skin and use electroreception to help them hunt small fish in the murky waters and flowing tides of their freshwater habitat.

GANGES SHARK ↘

Ganges sharks only live in freshwater ecosystems and are usually found in rivers around India, Nepal, Pakistan, Borneo and Myanmar. These critically endangered sharks grow up to 2m in length, and have a short broad snout with a wide mouth and tiny eyes. They hunt for bony fish and freshwater rays on the river floor and travel up to 100km in search of food.

FACT THE **VERY FIRST SHARKS** TO EXIST ON EARTH – AROUND 450 MILLION YEARS AGO – WERE **FRESHWATER** SHARKS.

THE WORLD'S
STRANGEST SHARKS

There are some weird, wild and wonderful sharks swimming in oceans all over the world. Let's take a look at some of the strangest!

NAME Goblin shark
HOTSPOTS Coastal Japan, Gulf of Mexico, southern tip of Brazil
FAVE FOOD Squid, dragonfish

This 125 million-year-old species might have been named after goblins in traditional Japanese folklore, but we think it looks like something way more alien. The goblin shark creeps up on dragonfish and squid, before firing pink jaws almost 8cm out of its mouth to snatch prey and scoff it down! Then it crams its jaws back inside its mouth like a grandpa putting his dentures back in... Flaps of skin retract, and in it goes. It's totally terrifying!

BIG NOSE!

GOBLIN SHARK? MORE LIKE 'GOBBLING' SHARK! *HIC!*

NAME Spotted wobbegong
HOTSPOTS Southern and western Australian reefs, the Indian ocean
FAVE FOOD Octopus, crabs, bony fish

Like its tasselled cousin, this strange shark is skilled in the art of camouflage and has beautiful patterning that earned it the nickname carpet shark. Its funny-sounding name is the Aboriginal word for 'shaggy beard', which perfectly describes the 24–26 pairs of lobes that branch out from the front of the shark's head to its pectoral fins. They act as sensors and scoop up passing fish straight into the shark's mouth.

Wobbegongs are sluggish sharks that only come out to feed at night. They can be found chilling in caves and under ocean shelves during the day – it's lucky they don't need to move to keep breathing!

FACT THERE ARE **12 DIFFERENT TYPES** OF WOBBEGONG, INCLUDING THE TASSELLED AND JAPANESE SPECIES.

NAME Horn shark
HOTSPOTS Coastal California and Mexico
FAVE FOOD Sea urchins, crabs, small fish, starfish

These cute little fellas are quiet, laidback and content to spend their days hidden in the shallow rock crevices of kelp forests before coming out at night to hunt. But horn sharks are pretty clumsy swimmers, so they've adapted to use their fins to help them crawl along the seabed. Compared with the whale shark – the world's largest fish species, which can reach 18m long – the horn shark is just a little tiddler at around 1m.

JUST CRAWLING MY WAY HOME TO CHILL OUT!

FACT HORN SHARKS ARE AN OVIPAROUS SPECIES – THEY **LAY SPIRAL-SHAPED EGGS** THAT LOOK LIKE SHELLS. PUPS HATCH AROUND NINE MONTHS LATER AND ARE JUST 15CM LONG.

25221. Neg Em 34455

FACT SOME COOKIECUTTERS' FINS AND COLLARS **GLOW BRIGHT GREEN**, BUT NOT THIS ONE!

NAME Cookiecutter shark
HOTSPOTS Tropical waters worldwide, from the Atlantic to the Pacific oceans
FAVE FOOD Squid, crabs, great white sharks, seals, orcas

Small they might be, but cookiecutter sharks will chomp on anything – from tiny critters to even scary apex hunters such as the great white sometimes. And don't be fooled by the sweet name – it describes the shark's feeding technique of gouging round plugs of flesh from its victims as though using a cookiecutter! Long-distance swimmers have also been nibbled at by this naughty shark.

OPEN WIDE!

Chances are you'd be pretty spooked if you saw a basking shark's mahoosive metre-wide mouth gaping your way. But these gentle giants, who cruise the British coastline between April and October, are the safest shark species to bump into. Ready to bask in their glory?

MOUTH

These stripes are actually specially adapted bones called gill-rakers.
   Made from strong but flexible cartilage, these bristle-like structures act like a giant sieve, trapping minute zooplankton!

CAN FILTER 3 SWIMMING POOLS' WORTH OF WATER PER HOUR

BRAIN

It might be the world's second-biggest fish, but the basking shark's brain is roughly the size of two matchboxes. The vital scent of zooplankton is picked up by a larger nerve centre wrapped around the brain.

THINK SMALL

The Scottish poet Norman MacCaig once described the basking shark as 'that room-sized monster with a matchbox brain'. How rude! They're not hunters, so they simply don't need the brainpower of a great white.

TEETH

In total, 1,500 teeny tiny hook-shaped teeth line six rows inside the upper jaw and nine rows along the lower jaw.

CAN LIVE FOR
50
YEARS

Stinky business

You'll get a whiff of the basking shark waaaaaaay before you see it. Their skin produces a mucus-based slime to put pesky parasites such as lamprey fish and other freeloaders off hitching a ride! It smells a little like ammonia, which is the eye-watering ingredient in lots of cleaning products. Yikes!

UTERUS

Females can be pregnant for up to three and a half years before giving birth to their young. That's a long time to wait!

LIVER

This huge, enlarged organ is flooded with energy-giving oil and acts as a buoyancy aid. Without it, this shark would sink!

What's in a name?

Once called sun sharks because people thought they were having a cheeky sunbathe, basking sharks come close to the water's surface to pick up delicious plankton.

Hunted!

Squalene, which is found in the basking shark's liver, was once used to make perfume, man-made silk and industrial lubricants. This made the creatures a target for fishermen before protective measures made the practice illegal.

SPENDS WEEKS SWIMMING AT A
DEPTH OF
1,000M

HIGH *flyers*

Welcome to South Africa's Seal Island, where great white sharks show off a special trick known as **breaching**. Want to learn more about this one giant leap for shark-kind?

SOUTH AFRICA

CAPE TOWN

SEAL ISLAND

Soaring species

Not all sharks can soar through the air. But basking, blacktip, shortfin mako, spinner and thresher sharks can all breach, thanks to the placement, power and shape of their fins!

40KM/H
SPEED OF GREAT WHITE BREACH

SHARK ASCENTS START
30 METRES BELOW THE SURFACE

LIGHT RELIEF

The second-largest shark, the basking shark, also breaches, but scientists aren't sure why. One theory is it removes itchy parasites from its skin by shocking them with a breach. Get off!

Spyhopping

As well as breaching, sharks love to peak over the waves to get a better look! This is called spyhopping and is all about being nosy. Sharks stick their heads up above the surface so they can see what's going on up there.

Breach for the stars

Every year Discovery hosts *Air Jaws: Ultimate Breach Off from Seal Island*. Fin-loving fanatics come and compete in False Bay to take the best breaching pic. In 2020 shark expert Chris Fallows snapped the highest ever caught on camera – a whopping 4.5m!

Sneaking up on seals

Breaching is brutal but crafty! Every sun-worshipping species is up for grabs, from sea lions and seals to turtles. Beneath the ocean's surface is always a blind spot for unsuspecting swimmers.

Flirting and flying

Some species dance to attract admirers, and scientists think basking sharks might breach to find a mate!

63

MARINE MATES

Sharks are mostly solitary creatures, but they're not always on their own. These apex predators also hang out with the odd pal or two... Would you like to be introduced?

The sucker on the head of a remora fish

Two parasite remora fish on a nurse shark

REMARKABLE REMORAS ↑

These critters are also known as suckerfish, as they have a special suction cup on top of their head. Remoras don't have a swim bladder, which is what many bony fish use to control how they float. So they attach themselves to sharks using their sucker and hitch a ride with them!

There are eight different species of remoras, and these thin, dark fish live in tropical and subtropical oceans and seas. Most remoras are around 45cm, but they range in length from 30 to 90cm, depending on their species. Their suction cup is a round disc-shaped plate on their head, which uses flexible membranes to grip surfaces. These fish don't just use sharks like underwater taxis, though...

When their hosts feed, the remoras detach and hoover up any leftovers. Plus, they help by eating any parasites or dead skin on their host's body – yum! Scientists believe there's an understanding between remoras and their shark hosts. Both know they benefit from their connection with each other, and it's thought this is why sharks don't gobble up their fishy hitchhikers.

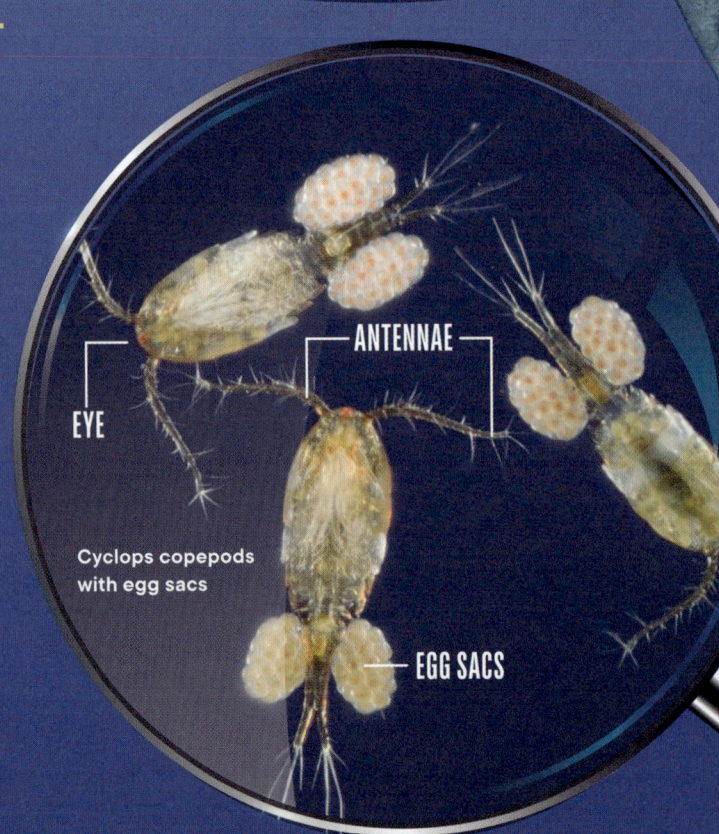

ANTENNAE

EYE

Cyclops copepods with egg sacs

EGG SACS

◀ Whale shark and golden trevally (aka pilot fish)

PLUCKY PILOT FISH ←

Unlike remoras, which attach themselves to sharks to get about, pilot fish swim alongside their shark friends to protect themselves from predators. In return for the sharks' bodyguard duties, the pilot fish eat parasites off their host, and clear up after their shark buddy has eaten by nibbling any leftovers. This special friendship (known as a mutualistic symbiotic relationship – phew!) is why sharks don't eat their pilot fish friends. Not even when the smaller fish swim into their gaping mouths to clean leftover pieces of food from between the shark's teeth!

Found in tropical and subtropical waters around the world, pilot fish are usually around 40cm long and have six or seven vertical stripes on their body that fade as the fish age.

▲ Pilot fish gathered round an oceanic whitetip shark

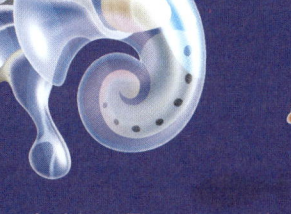

COOL COPEPODS ←

Not so much a friend as a surprise guest, copepods are a type of parasite that live on large sharks. These small, shrimp-like crustaceans are found in the fins, gills, nose, teeth and even eyeballs of pelagic (or ocean-dwelling) sharks such as great whites, hammerheads and shortfin makos.

Measuring just millimetres, copepods are often referred to as fish lice or 'insects of the sea'. They're an important part of the aquatic food chain that've been around more than 110 million years.

Distant cousins of crabs and lobsters, they're found in nearly every fresh and saltwater

habitat. They live anywhere it's wet – from bogs and marshes to lakes, oceans and even hot volcanic pools.

These watery fleas usually have a single eye in the centre of their head and two pairs of antennae, which is why they're often described as cyclops. Copepods have shells that are so thin, they're transparent, so it's possible to see inside their body. They're usually around 1-2mm long, but parasitic species can grow up to 32cm!

There are more than 13,000 species of copepods, and around a fifth of them are parasites.

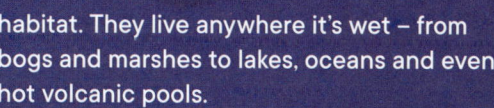

RAYS ARE SHARKS...

or are they?

Some shark features are so sweet, their close relatives share them. Let's shine a ray of light on these cartilaginous cousins!

MY COUSIN CYNTHIA IS A GREAT WHITE!

The family resemblance might not be obvious, but rays and sharks are closely related. Both are cartilaginous fish, which means their skeletons are made of flexible cartilage (the bendy tissue found in your ears and nose) rather than bone. And with more than 600 different species found around the world, rays are the most diverse group of such fish. Different types include stingrays, electric rays, manta rays, skates and sawfish. Unlike sharks, rays have wide, flat, disc-shaped bodies. Many species have a long, whip-like tail, which often has one or more sharp, saw-edged, venomous spines. These graceful movers swim either by flapping their wing-like pectoral fins or moving their whole body in a wavy motion.

STINGRAYS ←

Fossils reveal that stingrays have been around since the Lower Jurassic period some 150 million years ago. These guys are usually grey, which helps them blend in with the seafloor and avoid predators such as sharks and larger rays. If stingrays do feel threatened, they defend themselves by lashing out with their long, jagged tail. It often has a poisonous sharp stinger at the end, so watch out!

Stingrays spend a lot of time partially buried in sand, either sleeping, hiding from predators or waiting to ambush prey. Their eyes perch on top of their heads so they can craftily keep watch while they're buried.

Like some other rays, stingrays have electrical sensors on their face to help detect potential prey. These electroreceptors are another thing they have in common with sharks.

Stingrays' mouths are underneath their body – something that comes in handy for gobbling crabs, clams, snails and shrimp from the seabed.

SOME OF THE LARGER RAYS NEVER STOP SWIMMING!

LAST NIGHT I THOUGHT I WAS BEING CHASED BY A SHARK...

THIS MORNING, I REALISED IT WAS JUST A 'BREAM'!

FACT SOME RAYS USE THEIR BLUNT TEETH TO **CRUSH THEIR PREY**.

EATS

SKATES →

EGG CASE

These rays are a similar shape to stingrays, but they have a shorter, thicker tail and don't have a stinger. Skates hunt for food on the seabed and eat worms, small fish, crabs and molluscs, such as clams, oysters and mussels... A bottom-feeder's buffet!

Most rays are ovoviviparous – meaning they give birth to live young (known as pups) – but skates are different because they produce eggs. Their dark, rectangular egg cases are up to 10cm long and have long, horn-like projections on each corner. These 'horns' help them attach to seaweed or other objects on the seafloor. After 3–15 months, the case opens and a fully formed young skate emerges. Empty skate egg cases wash up on the beach, just as sharks' do.

EATS

FACT AS WELL AS USING THEIR GILLS, **RAYS BREATHE** THROUGH TWO **SMALL HOLES** BEHIND THEIR EYES, THE SAME WAY SHARKS DO!

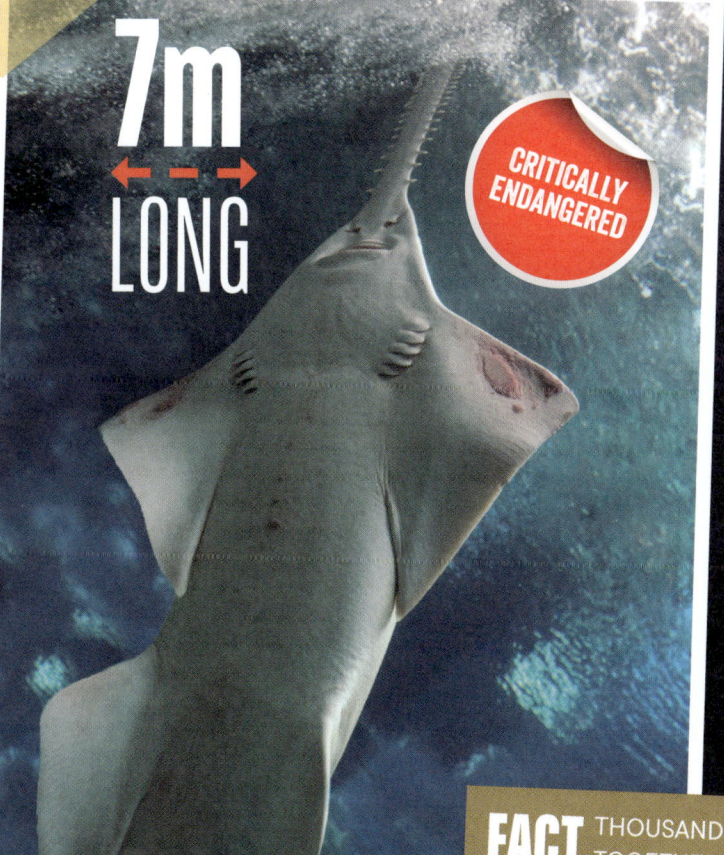

7m LONG

CRITICALLY ENDANGERED

SAWFISH ←

These rays are among the largest fish in the world and are easy to identify thanks to their long, flat nose. Their distinctive snout is called a rostrum and has strong teeth on each side, which makes it look like a saw. Like some sharks, sawfish use their rostrum to sense and stun prey, and to defend themselves from predators such as crocodiles.

Sawfish look similar to their sawshark relations but – as with other rays – their gills are underneath their body, rather than on the side of their head like sharks' are.

Each and every type – the largetooth sawfish, smalltooth sawfish, green sawfish, dwarf sawfish and narrow sawfish – can be found throughout the world in tropical and subtropical waters. Sadly, sawfish are the most threatened rays on the planet, with all five species now listed as endangered.

Some sawfish species are larger than great white sharks, growing up to 7m long!

FACT THOUSANDS OF RAYS **MIGRATE** TO FEEDING GROUNDS TOGETHER IN GROUPS KNOWN AS **FEVERS**.

MEGA MANTAS

Ray to go!
Get ready to
dip into some
magnificent facts
about manta rays

▶ Manta rays are mostly black and
have diamond-shaped bodies. They're
famous for moving gracefully as they
swim, using their pectoral fins as
'wings' to glide through the water

More mantas

Scientists originally thought there was
just one species of manta ray, but in 2008
they discovered there are actually two. Meet the
giant oceanic manta ray and the reef manta ray.

Giant oceanic manta rays live in the world's
major oceans and spend most of their time far from land,
searching for food in the depths of their watery world. Reef
manta rays are smaller, and live in tropical and subtropical
coastal areas in the Indian and Pacific oceans.

Both species of manta ray look similar but their size makes it
easy to tell them apart. Reef manta rays are usually around 3m
wide, while giant oceanic manta rays are much bigger. In fact,
giant oceanic manta rays are the world's largest ray species.
They have a wingspan of around 7m and can weigh as much
as 2,000kg – which is as heavy as a rhinoceros!

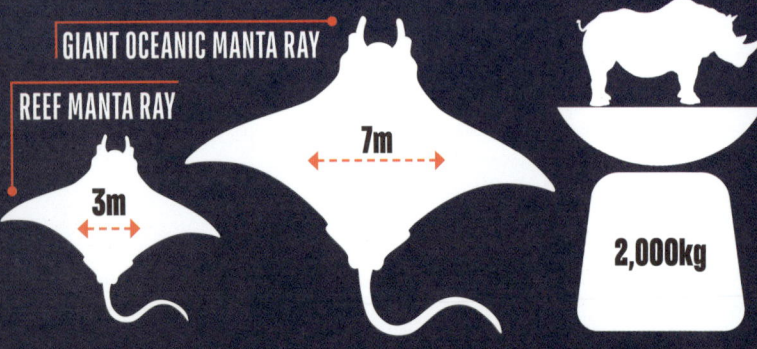

GIANT OCEANIC MANTA RAY
REEF MANTA RAY
3m
7m
2,000kg

▲ It might look like rays have a funny
face on their underside, but those
'eyes' are actually spiracles that help
them breathe

Brilliant brains

These beautiful swimmers are
super-clever and have the biggest
brains of any fish. Research has
shown mantas are some of the
smartest creatures in the ocean.
They recognise themselves in
reflections, use smell and sight
to map their environment, seek
help if they get tangled in fishing
lines and have impressive
long-term memories.

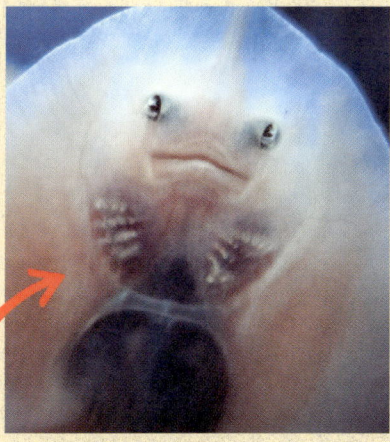

Perfect pups

Like most rays, mantas are ovoviviparous. Their young hatch from an egg inside the mother, and well-developed pups are born looking like mini-versions of adults. Manta rays produce one pup at a time, which takes around 13 months to develop. Pups already have a huge wingspan of 1.5m when they're born, but they grow slowly and it takes 10 years for them to become adults.

SPECIAL STATIONS

Manta rays make sure they stay healthy with regular visits to cleaning stations. These are areas in coral reefs where small fish – often wrasses and angelfish – remove parasites and dead skin from the manta's gills, teeth and skin. Um... yum?

AAAAALLLL ABOARD!

Cephalic snacks

Mantas have special fins called cephalic lobes on either side of their long mouths. These flexible fins earned rays the nickname devilfish because they look like horns. The fins help mantas direct food and water into their mouths.

Manta rays are filter feeders, meaning they swim with their mouths open and pass water and food through their gills. The seawater passes through, and tasty food is caught and eaten.

These deep-sea divers eat around 30kg of food each day. And when mantas discover an area with plenty of plankton or krill, they often do somersaults to help them stay in one place so they can eat more of their favourite food!

When threatened, manta rays can reach speeds of up to 24km/h as they race to escape danger!

▲ Potential meals: enter here!

CHIMAERA
cousins

These deep-sea divers are closely related to rays, sharks and skates. Come and meet the chimaera

Fantastic fish

Also known as rat fish, elephant fish and rabbit fish, scientists think chimaeras first appeared in our oceans more than 400 million years ago. These amazing creatures range from 60–200cm and have cartilaginous skeletons – just like their shark relatives. But, although they're similar to sharks, chimaeras have some big differences. Their upper jaw is fused to their skull, they have four gills that are hidden by soft coverings on each side of their body and three sets of permanent grinding plates instead of teeth.

Just like sharks, chimaeras have a special network of sensors called a lateral line system, which uses the tiniest hair cells to detect vibrations and movement

Where in the world?

Chimaeras are found in oceans all over the world, apart from the Arctic and Antarctic. Although a few species prefer to live in shallow coastal areas, most chimaeras are found out in the ocean at depths of 200 to 2,600m – so, very close to the seafloor.

The rabbit fish may not look big, but it can grow to 1.5m

in the water. They're sometimes known as ghost sharks, but these multicoloured marvels are anything but. The chimaeras are survivors of the sea.

Spotted ▼
rat fish

ANCIENT!

Like skates and some shark species, **chimaeras** reproduce by **laying eggs**. Females lay **two eggs** at the same time, and it takes between **six and 12 months** for their pups to **hatch**

More than 50 species of chimaera have been discovered and divided into three groups, based on the shape of their snouts...

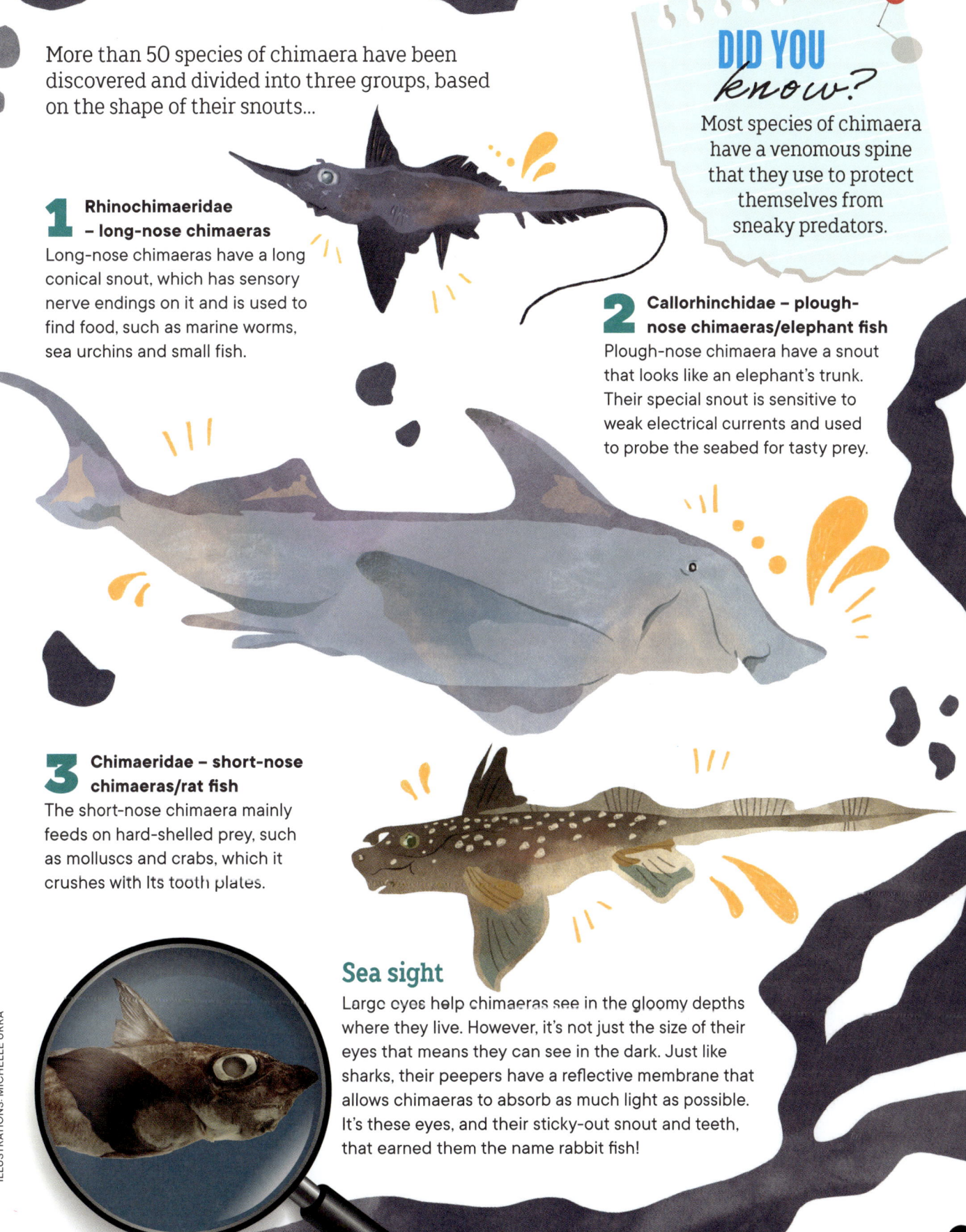

DID YOU *know?*

Most species of chimaera have a venomous spine that they use to protect themselves from sneaky predators.

1 Rhinochimaeridae – long-nose chimaeras

Long-nose chimaeras have a long conical snout, which has sensory nerve endings on it and is used to find food, such as marine worms, sea urchins and small fish.

2 Callorhinchidae – plough-nose chimaeras/elephant fish

Plough-nose chimaera have a snout that looks like an elephant's trunk. Their special snout is sensitive to weak electrical currents and used to probe the seabed for tasty prey.

3 Chimaeridae – short-nose chimaeras/rat fish

The short-nose chimaera mainly feeds on hard-shelled prey, such as molluscs and crabs, which it crushes with its tooth plates.

Sea sight

Large eyes help chimaeras see in the gloomy depths where they live. However, it's not just the size of their eyes that means they can see in the dark. Just like sharks, their peepers have a reflective membrane that allows chimaeras to absorb as much light as possible. It's these eyes, and their sticky-out snout and teeth, that earned them the name rabbit fish!

RECORD BREAKERS!

Not all species are created equal! Each shark is remarkable, but this lot really chomped their way into the record books

AT LEAST $8,000,000!

MOST EXPENSIVE SHARK? ⬆

Do you think this pickled shark is art? Damien Hirst does! In 1991, the British artist preserved a tiger shark in a solution containing formaldehyde. The piece, titled *The Physical Impossibility of Death in the Mind of Someone Living*, cost £50,000 to make and was sold in 2004 for an undisclosed sum reported to be 'at least' $8 million!

FIRST SHARK ⬅

Meet the earliest identifiable shark... We think it looks pretty good for 360 MILLION years old. There's still some debate about whether the extinct Cladoselache is a shark or a distant relative, but this is definitely the species the fantastic feature set of today's sharks can be traced back to.

CLADOSELACHE FOSSILS WERE **FIRST FOUND** IN **LAKE ERIE IN 1894**. THAT'S A LONG TIME TO GO UNDISCOVERED!

HOW LONG HAS THIS FISHY HOUSEGUEST OUTSTAYED HIS WELCOME? →

If you're ever in Oxford, don't be surprised to find a larger-than-life great white sticking out of someone's house! The Headington Shark first made headlines in 1986, when it was created to spark a conversation about conservation. Its owner Bill Heine fought for years to keep his fibreglass friend up on the roof.

LIKE MANY SPECIES, THE SANDBAR IS MOST THREATENED BY HUMANS. BUT THIS SHARK PREFERS TO USE ITS FANGS ON BONY FISH SUCH AS **CROAKERS AND SNAPPERS**

SHARPEST TEETH →

The sandbar shark's teeth really are cracking. At 2.5cm each, they might not be the largest of shark teeth, but come in multiple rows of up to 17 that crunch through even the hardiest crustacean shells with ease. Feeling hungry?

73

6,000 NEWTONS OF FORCE

MOST POWERFUL JAWS

The great white is considered great for many reasons, but it's not the best at taking a bite. That title was snatched by the bull shark. The fierce force of its jaw is almost 6,000 newtons – far more than this champion chomper needs for the marine life on its menu.

80km/h

FASTEST SHARK

The shortfin mako is one of the fastest fish in the ocean, and it's certainly the speediest shark around. It's an endotherm, meaning it regulates its blood temperature to keep its streamlined body ready for action. Sure, it could win any race, but imagine it hunting! On land, it's faster than a greyhound at full speed – so this grey-skinned shark can really move.

3½ YEARS

ITS SPECIES NAME, **ANGUINEUS**, TRANSLATES AS **'CONSISTING OF SNAKES'** – THIS SHARK IS SERIOUSLY SLIPPERY!

LONGEST TIME PREGNANT

If you think people spend ages pregnant, then you won't believe how long the frilled shark has to wait to have babies! Three-and-a-half years is longer than any other creature with a backbone spends waiting to give birth. Taking so long to meet their pups puts these sharks at real risk of harm from human fishing practices.

18m

BIGGEST EVER SHARK

The megalodon wasn't just the biggest species of its time – it was the largest predatory shark ever! It could grow up to 18m and had a 3.4m-wide mouth. JAWsome!

CHAPTER 3
SHARKS AND US

It's fair to say that humans and sharks are a little wary of each other – but are we right to be cautious? Do they want to harm us? Where does this distrust come from? And what does the future hold? Read on for some answers...

MISTAKEN IDENTITY?

Almost half the UK has galeophobia – a fear of sharks. It might help to understand the reasons behind their rare attacks on humans – and why we've got nothing to worry about in our part of the world

In 1891 a banker named Hermann Oelrichs offered a large reward to anyone who could prove that a shark attack had occurred off the east coast of the US. No one came forward.

However, in the summer of 1916, three people were killed and another injured along the coast of New Jersey. A single great white shark was thought to be the culprit, but recent studies suggest it was more likely a bull shark – or even more than one shark. The attacks did, however, provide the inspiration for the 1975 movie *Jaws* – they even get a mention in the film.

There might be a greater chance of getting hurt while driving to the seaside or being carried away by strong currents in the water, but the fact is sharks do occasionally attack humans. Here we take a closer look at why these rare occurrences sometimes happen.

WHY DO SHARKS ATTACK?

1 **MISTAKEN IDENTITY**
Picking the wrong target is a particular problem for great white sharks. Because this species usually attacks from below the surface, someone in a dark wet suit lying on a surfboard might look like regular prey to a great white at such an angle. These attacks include what scientists call 'bite and spit' – the shark, mistakenly believing it's attacking a seal or sea lion, makes a charge from beneath, takes one big bite then moves off to let the prey weaken. Mistaken identity often occurs in murky water. Off the coast of Florida, people sometimes get bitten by small sharks hunting fish close to shore. The shark sees skin on the palm of the hand or sole of the foot, which is usually much paler than the tanned outer areas, and mistakes the human for a fish. Usually the bite is swift and only leaves a few scratches. In some cases, swimmers aren't even aware of the bite until later!

2 **BUMPS AND BITES** These aren't necessarily meant as attacks. If sharks get curious about something in or on the water, they may approach using their mouths to test what's there and whether it's edible. Many surfboards have been 'toothed' by a shark, only for it to swim off after finding the board's not that tasty.

"TOOTHED" SURF BOARD

3 **DEFENCE** This sort of attack usually occurs on reefs. Sharks that live on coral reefs are often small and, if a snorkeller or diver approaches such a shark, it can feel nervous or threatened. The shark will swim in a very exaggerated manner – with its back arched and its pectoral fins lowered – as a warning to the person, who may not be familiar with the signal and keep approaching. This can trigger an attack, which is usually a single quick bite.

4 **TERRITORIAL DEFENCE** Similar to the self-defence described above, this sort of attack usually takes place on reefs where sharks defend their feeding grounds. A snorkeller or diver could be seen as a competing predator so the shark attacks to drive off the intruder.

WHITETIP SHARK

5 **FEEDING** Very occasionally, an attack is motivated by hunger. This is most likely to happen where you are least likely to be – in the middle of the ocean. Sharks such as the oceanic whitetip live out there in what might be called a desert of water. The chances to feed are few and far between, so anything they encounter must be treated as a potential meal. Such sharks become super-aggressive as a result and a threat to anyone unlucky enough to find themselves in the water miles out to sea.

HOW TO AVOID A SHARK ATTACK

Follow this guide when you're swimming in seas where potentially dangerous sharks might be.
So that's nowhere in the UK, then!

* **Ask about the area** you're going to swim in, especially whether it has a history of shark attacks.

* **Learn about shark behaviour.** In certain areas, such as coral reefs, sharks may see you as a threat to their feeding grounds and to themselves. Learn to recognise the way a shark swims when it's feeling defensive (see opposite). Look out for arched backs and lowered pectoral fins. If you see this behaviour in any shark, back off!

* **Sharks usually feed at particular times,** so try not to swim at night or at dawn or dusk.

* **Be aware of other animals in the sea.** If fish dart about or disappear, it might mean a predator is nearby.

* **Give murky waters a wide berth.** If you're in a place known for shark attacks, stay away from water with poor visibility. It's far easier for a case of mistaken identity to happen here – for humans *and* sharks.

* **Wear sunscreen.** Yep, think about your skin! Remember, having a tan can make the palms of your hands and soles of your feet stand out underwater. A hand flapping about can look like a fish and attract a hungry shark, so wear dark gloves and swimming shoes.

* **If you're at the seaside**, don't swim too far out.

* **Don't swim alone**, even if there aren't any sharks about.

* **But don't go swimming with dogs or horses, either**! Animals can attract sharks.

* **Steer clear of any river mouths and channels** in the seabed where the water becomes deeper. Sharks regularly swim around such spots.

* **Always listen to lifeguards.** If they tell you to leave the water, then leave the water!

* **If you see a shark**, leave them alone! They're usually minding their own business. Don't bother them and they won't bother you.

* **If in doubt... STAY OUT!**

ILLUSTRATIONS: MICHELLE URRA

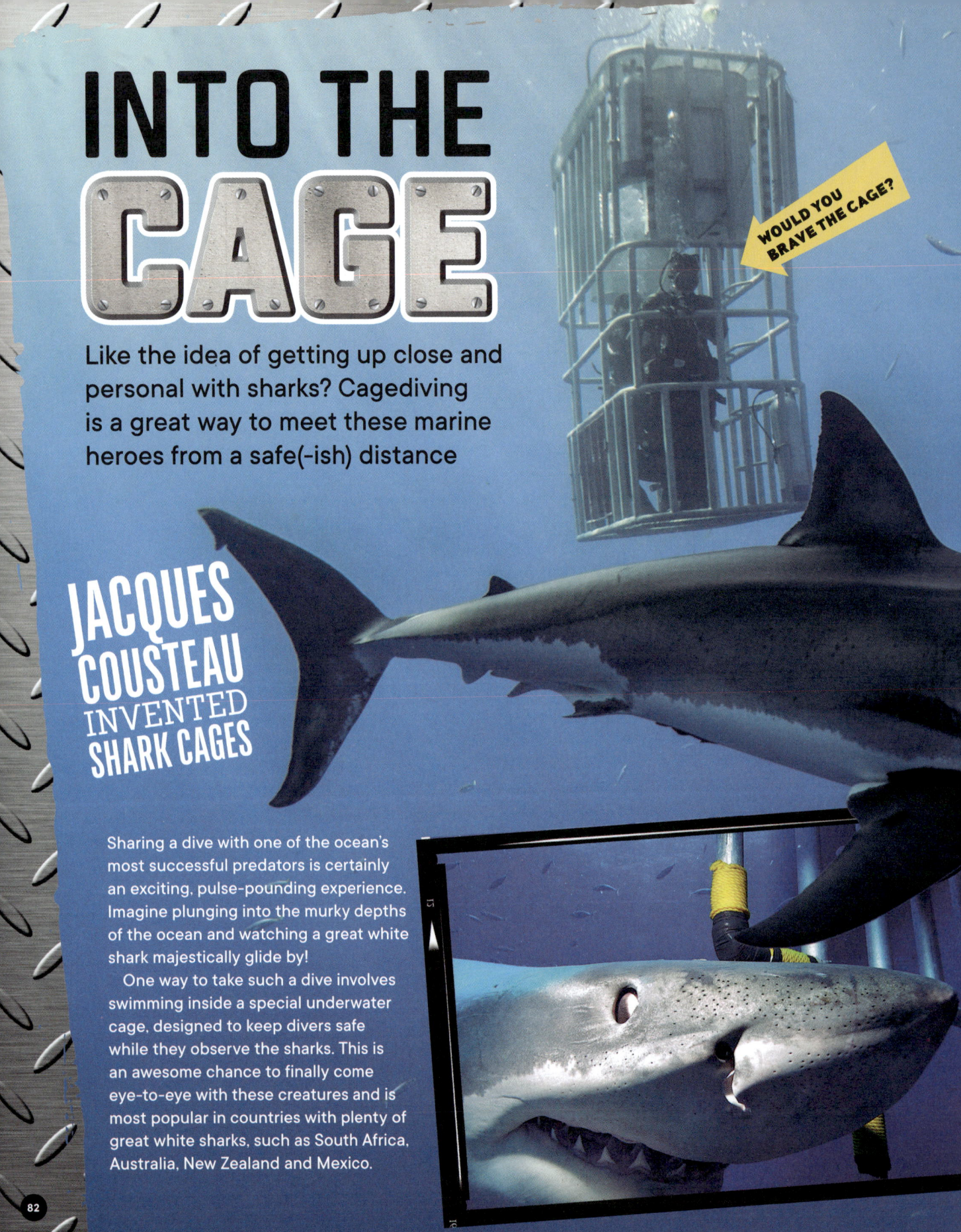

INTO THE
CAGE

Like the idea of getting up close and personal with sharks? Cagediving is a great way to meet these marine heroes from a safe(-ish) distance

WOULD YOU BRAVE THE CAGE?

JACQUES COUSTEAU INVENTED SHARK CAGES

Sharing a dive with one of the ocean's most successful predators is certainly an exciting, pulse-pounding experience. Imagine plunging into the murky depths of the ocean and watching a great white shark majestically glide by!

One way to take such a dive involves swimming inside a special underwater cage, designed to keep divers safe while they observe the sharks. This is an awesome chance to finally come eye-to-eye with these creatures and is most popular in countries with plenty of great white sharks, such as South Africa, Australia, New Zealand and Mexico.

Cage construction

Modern shark cages are made out of aluminium – the same stuff used in kitchen foil, tin cans and window frames. This metal is perfect for shark cages because it's strong, flexible and doesn't rust in water. Aluminium is also one of the lightest metals in the world, which means that today's cages are much easier to handle than some of the earlier versions.

Shark cages are attached to a boat and lowered into the water. They're usually big enough to fit four divers at a time, and are designed with large openings that offer the best view of any nearby sharks. A lot of modern cages use a hookah system, which pumps air from the boat to each diver through a single hose fitted to their mask. This means the less experienced can cage dive because they don't need to know how to use scuba diving equipment.

SOME CAGE DIVERS USE FROZEN FISH TO ATTRACT SHARKS. BAITING THEM THIS WAY

ISN'T ILLEGAL, BUT IT IS CONTROVERSIAL

AS IT'S THOUGHT TO ALTER THE NATURAL BEHAVIOUR OF SHARKS

COOL CONSERVATION

Shark cage diving isn't just used to see these fascinating fish in their natural habitat. It's also an important part of understanding and protecting them. These special cages have played an important role in shark conservation, as they make it much easier to study these beautiful beasts. And the more we understand them, the more we understand the threats they face. Data gathered from shark research is used to influence changes in the law that help protect sharks and ensure their future.

Cage creation

These clever contraptions were invented by the undersea explorer Jacques Cousteau to assist his scientific research on sharks. He created the world's first shark cage when he was making a film called *The Silent World* in 1956.

Then, in the 1960s, Australian conservationist Rodney Fox came up with a new, improved shark cage design. Inspired by a visit to Australia's Adelaide Zoo, the steel cages he built were more secure. Rodney's first design has been updated throughout the years, but today's cages are still based on his original model.

WHAT'S IT LIKE BEING AN...
AQUARIST?

interview

Welcome to the world's oldest aquarium! For 150 years, SEA LIFE Brighton has been at the forefront of marine conservation, including shark welfare. There are more than 3,500 species here, and Joe Williams works tirelessly to make sure they're happy and healthy

Joe Williams, Curator

What is an
AQUARIST?

Joe's role as an aquarist is proof that you really can turn your dream into a dream job! An aquarist cares for all the animals in an aquarium by making sure their living environments stay in tip-top condition and that each species gets a healthy, balanced diet and lots of attention!

READY FOR ANYTHING At an aquarium, no two days are the same – it's one of the reasons Joe loves working with marine life. Even in the time *Factology* got to spend with Joe at the aquarium, staff needed his input to make sure everything was running smoothly. The inhabitants rely on a team of experts working together – from engineers and vets to the staff that welcome visitors when they arrive. Joe's job is important, so he lives close by to make sure he's always on hand – 24 hours a day.

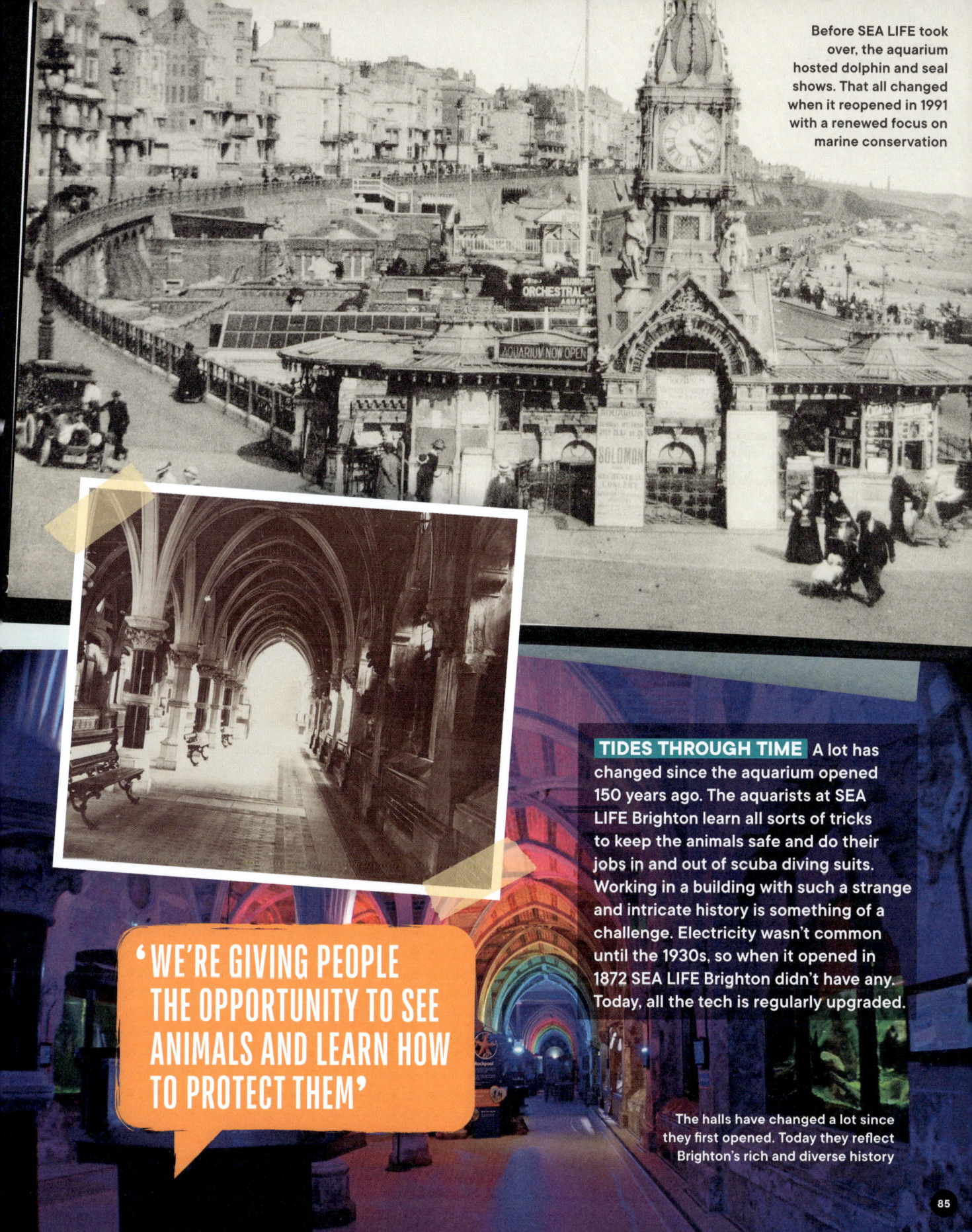

Before SEA LIFE took over, the aquarium hosted dolphin and seal shows. That all changed when it reopened in 1991 with a renewed focus on marine conservation

TIDES THROUGH TIME A lot has changed since the aquarium opened 150 years ago. The aquarists at SEA LIFE Brighton learn all sorts of tricks to keep the animals safe and do their jobs in and out of scuba diving suits. Working in a building with such a strange and intricate history is something of a challenge. Electricity wasn't common until the 1930s, so when it opened in 1872 SEA LIFE Brighton didn't have any. Today, all the tech is regularly upgraded.

'WE'RE GIVING PEOPLE THE OPPORTUNITY TO SEE ANIMALS AND LEARN HOW TO PROTECT THEM'

The halls have changed a lot since they first opened. Today they reflect Brighton's rich and diverse history

FISHY FOOD Ever wondered what these creatures eat? There's no live feeding in the aquarium (it's only fair to the food!), and data from scientists around the world help Joe and his team provide the perfect diet for all the species at SEA LIFE Brighton. Scientists reckon there are 8.7 million plant and animal species on the planet today – and every single one of them needs the right diet. From sustainably sourced fish to shortfin squid, it's a varied menu!

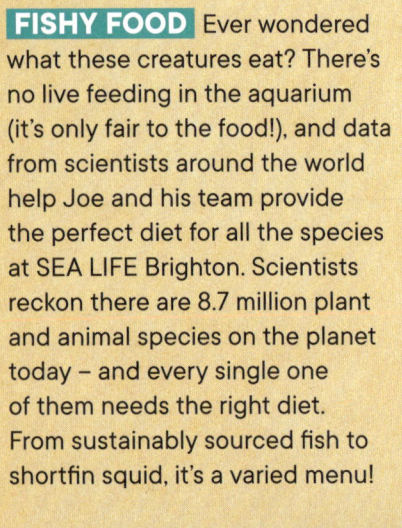

MEET DOTTY – SHE'S A ZEBRA SHARK!

Marine mates

Think sharks are stupid? Think again! One of Joe's favourite marine mates is Dotty, a zebra shark he swims with in the display. Dotty will play with Joe and even swim through his legs. That's one smart shark!

Joe and his staff regularly suit up in scuba gear to check on the animals and their displays

BRAIN TRAINING If you have a pet, you know there's more to looking after it than just feeding – you need to keep it entertained! In the aquarium, keeping animals active and engaged is called 'enrichment'. Joe organised the first aquarium enrichment workshop in the UK, which helps every animal reach their A-game. Staff love to train the animals and have even proved you can teach a shark when it's dinner time.

SAFE DISPLAYS How do you make sure aquarium water is safe for the fish? SEA LIFE Brighton sits on a massive reservoir of local sea water. The city's on the coast, so there's plenty of it! Careful science is used to make sure it's just right for every species so they can breathe easily. Staff dive in the displays every day to clean them, keep the animals active and make sure everything's safe. This job sounds so cool!

FACT WANT TO VISIT OR FIND OUT MORE ABOUT HOW THE SEA LIFE TRUST IS SAVING SHARKS? HEAD TO VISITSEALIFE.COM

SAFE AT SEA LIFE Specialist centres around the world help animals return to the wild, but the hardworking staff at SEA LIFE Brighton make sure their residents are in the safest place possible. People often ask Joe why they don't release their animals and his answer is simple: they're happy and healthy here. All the watery guys at SEA LIFE Brighton survive and thrive in this safe setting, without having to worry about becoming a tasty snack for bigger fish!

> **'HUMANS POSE A MUCH BIGGER RISK TO SHARKS THAN THEY DO TO US'**

Shark species to see up close at SEA LIFE Brighton:

* Blacktip reef shark
* Zebra shark
* Bull huss shark
* Lesser-spotted dogfish
* Bamboo shark

NEW FRIENDS The aquarists at SEA LIFE Brighton don't just look after the animals on display – they tend to some behind the scenes, too. In this setting, caring for these marine wonders is called 'husbandry' and it's led to plenty more fish to look after! Generations of blacktip reef sharks have grown up here. Aquarists welcomed the largest litter of blacktip reef sharks EVER in the UK – six shark pups were born in one go. That's incredible!

Don't judge a book by its cover – sharks really aren't that scary!

> **'ANY SHARK ATTACK IS A CASE OF MISTAKEN IDENTITY. THEY DON'T ACTIVELY HUNT HUMANS – OUR IRON-RICH BLOOD ISN'T A TASTY SNACK FOR THEM'**

SOS SAVE OUR SHARKS

Mankind's influence on marine life worldwide has often been harmful. Over the next few pages, we'll show you why sharks are under threat – and what can be done about it...

OCEAN ACIDIFICATION

We already know that sea water is salty and not safe for humans to drink, but imagine if it was no longer fit for fish! Ocean acidification is the chemical change in the sea's pH (potential hydration) levels – the lower the water's pH number, the worse it is for wildlife. Shell-forming animals like coral, crabs, oysters and urchins desperately rely on the healthy natural minerals in sea water.

So how deadly is acidification for sharks? It affects everything from their skin to their sense of smell. Worryingly, species such as clown fish wouldn't be able to find their way home or even breed without the latter.

Rising acid levels could cause delicate denticles and their tough teeth to corrode and dissolve, making feeding, hunting and even swimming difficult for sharks. We brush our teeth to stop sugar destroying our teeth. Sadly, sharks don't have that option.

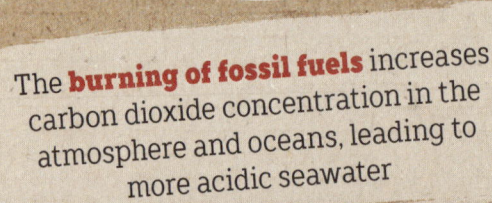

The **burning of fossil fuels** increases carbon dioxide concentration in the atmosphere and oceans, leading to more acidic seawater

The ocean is naturally balanced to preserve and protect marine species, including sharks. So how does climate change threaten their environment? The biggest problem is the rise in temperature caused by trapped greenhouse gases in our atmosphere. Scientists predict that by the year 2100, waters could be more than 2°C warmer as a result, which would make the world a much scarier place for sharks.

This might not sound like a big change, but can you imagine feeling too hot every single day? Sharks could be compelled to migrate to new areas where they might not survive. The sea's salinity could shift to dangerous levels and, if the amount of oxygen in the water is reduced, this could create 'dead spots' where it's no longer safe for certain species to live.

Heat-seeking species

In February 2022, there were reports of a great white shark spotted off the southeast coast of the UK. Don't panic! Nobody was hurt – but the arrival of unfamiliar fins on our shores has been blamed on the rise in temperatures caused by climate change. So many species featured in this book are drawn to tropical or 'temperate' waters. As ours warm up, they may find themselves wandering far from home.

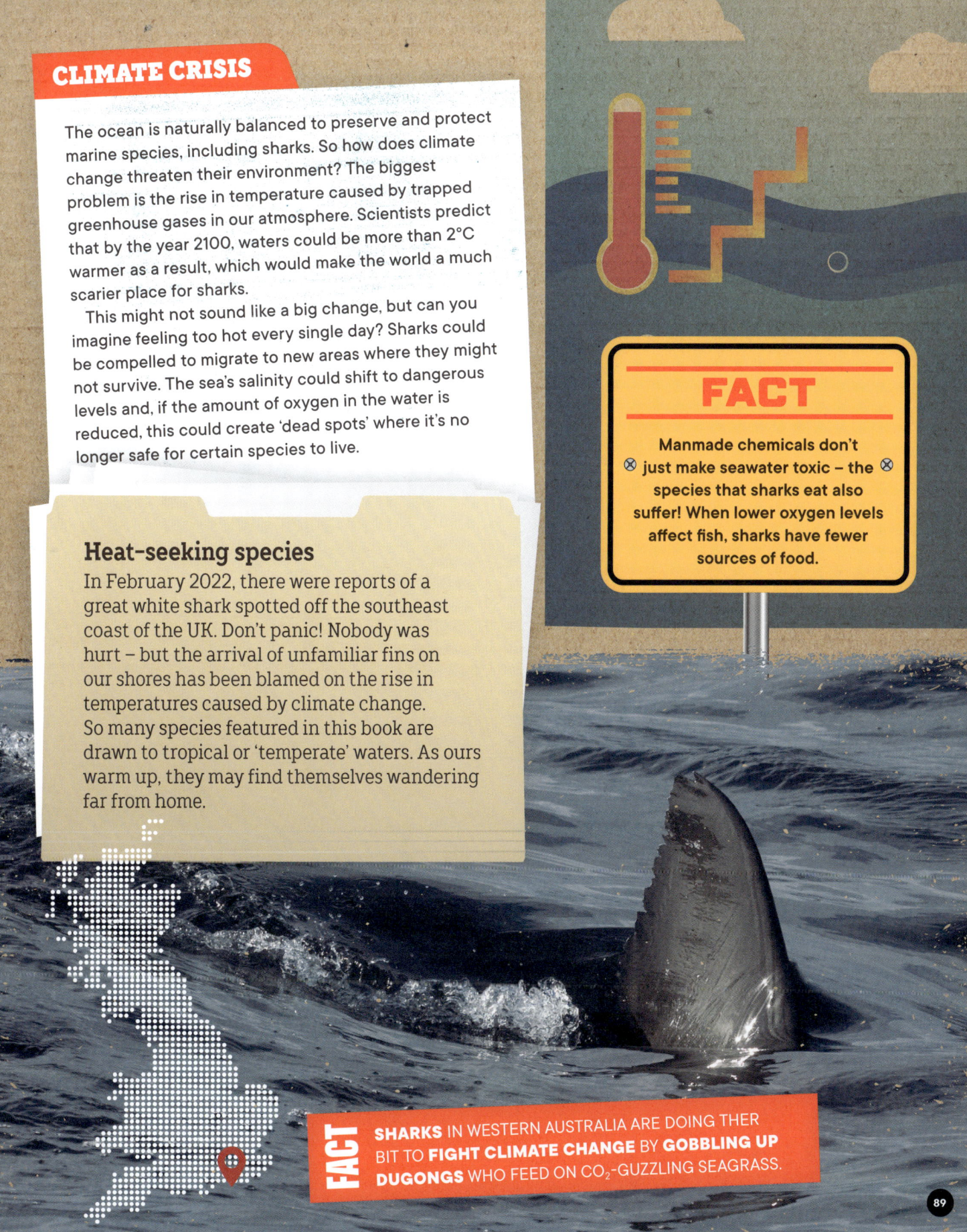

FACT

Manmade chemicals don't just make seawater toxic – the species that sharks eat also suffer! When lower oxygen levels affect fish, sharks have fewer sources of food.

FACT SHARKS IN WESTERN AUSTRALIA ARE DOING THEIR BIT TO **FIGHT CLIMATE CHANGE** BY **GOBBLING UP DUGONGS** WHO FEED ON CO_2-GUZZLING SEAGRASS.

67% OF SHARKS ARE CONTAMINATED WITH PLASTIC

PLASTIC AND POLLUTION

Plastic is a big problem for small fish – it's not just great whites chomping on coffee cups we have to worry about. Think about all those bottom-feeders – the marine animals that feed on things along the seafloor. Rubbish in the sea sinks to the places they hunt. For humans, it's easy to ignore, but fish aren't so lucky.

Researchers believe that, based on how many plastic-filled fish have been found, between 10–30% of fish will be contaminated with microplastics from old fishing gear or washing machines (and just general rubbish, such as wet wipes) that make it out to sea. If you're wondering why they eat pollutants, remember that fish aren't aware of how harmful some of the waste we let into their waters can be.

HOW PLASTIC ENTERS OUR FOODCHAIN

Small **pieces of plastic are swallowed** along with water and plankton by small fish, which are then eaten by other animals and so on...

FINNING AND FISHING

When humans enter the water, sharks cease to be at the top of its food chain! Some cultures still make shark-fin soup, a traditional stew that dates back more than 1,000 years. It remains a status symbol, even though the fin is so lacking in flavour that chicken stock is added. Without its fin, a shark can't swim so will sink and die. Fins are also popular in certain traditional medicines, despite often being toxic.

Thankfully, attitudes are changing around the world. Many companies and governments have banned fishing methods that put sharks at risk. Carelessness can cause sharks to get snared in nets and ropes even when they aren't being directly hunted by fishermen. Activists and charities are working hard to fight dangerous practices, but microplastics found in fishing equipment cause other problems for sharks.

FACT

100 million sharks are killed every year through over-fishing, finning, oceanic pollution and getting caught in lines and nets meant for other fish

FACT

SHARKS ACT AS CARBON SINKS BY CAPTURING CARBON IN THEIR POO SO IT ENDS UP ON THE SEABED RATHER THAN GETTING INTO THE ATMOSPHERE. SHARK POO ALSO MAKES GREAT FERTILISER FOR SHALLOW-WATER PLANTS!

THE BIG
SHARK QUIZ

Read the book, then put your knowledge to the test!

1 Which kind of fish make up approximately 95% of fish in the ocean? *(See p7)*

2 What shape is a great white shark's brain? *(See p8)*

3 What are the two types of muscles sharks have? *(See p9)*

4 What shape are bullshark eggs? *(See p21)*

5 How many dorsal fins do cow sharks have? *(See p42)*

6 To the nearest thousand, how many teeth can a great white have in its lifetime? *(See p47)*

7 What kills 100 million sharks every year? *(See p49)*

8 Up to how far will the great hammerhead shark migrate? *(See p51)*

9 How long was the largest whale shark ever recorded? *(See p52)*

10 How much water can a basking shark filter in an hour? *(See p60)*

11 Which species weighs as much as a rhinoceros? *(See p68)*

12 What is the Headington Shark made of? *(See p73)*

13 What is a fear of sharks called? *(See p76)*

14 Who invented the shark cage? *(See p83)*

15 What contaminates 67% of sharks? *(See p90)*

GLOSSARY

ALGAE
A type of plant, without leaves or stems, that grows in and near water.

AMMONIA
A colourless gas or liquid that has a strong smell and dissolves in water.

BASKING
Lying or relaxing in a warm, comfortable place.

BREACHING
To make an opening in something, such as the surface of water.

BUOYANCY
The ability to float in water or air.

CARNIVORE
An animal that eats meat.

CARRION
The decaying flesh of dead animals.

CARTILAGE
Strong but flexible material found in parts of the body.

ECOSYSTEM
Everything (living or inanimate) that exists in one place.

EMBRYO
An animal in the early stages of development before it is born.

FIN
A flipper that enables the fish to steer through water.

GALEOPHOBIA
A fear of sharks.

GILL
The organs through which fish breathe underwater.

HERBIVORE
An animal that only eats plants.

MAMMAL
An animal that feeds milk to its young and often has hair or fur.

MICROBE
A tiny living thing that can only be seen with a microscope.

OLFACTORY
A word for something connected with the sense of smell.

PARASITE
An animal or plant that lives on another animal or plant.

PLANKTON
Tiny animal and plant life that lives in water.

POLLUTION
A general term for what makes land, water or air dirty and unsuitable to use.

PREDATOR
An animal that lives by killing and eating other animals.

SERRATED
To have an edge with a row of small teeth.

SYMBIOTIC
A word used to describe the relationship between two kinds of living things that depend on each other.

VENOMOUS
The ability to poison another animal by bite or sting.

VENTILATION
The process that allows fresh air to enter a space or body.

ZOOPLANKTON
Plankton that are animals.

QUIZ ANSWERS

1. Bony fish
2. Y-shaped (with two bulbs!)
3. White and red
4. Spiral-shaped
5. One
6. 30,000
7. Fishing practices
8. Up to 1,200km
9. 18.8m long
10. Three swimming pools' worth!
11. Giant oceanic manta ray
12. Fibreglass
13. Galeophobia
14. Jacques Cousteau
15. Plastic

INDEX

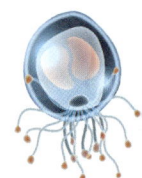

First published 2024 by Button Books, an imprint of Guild of Master Craftsman Publications Ltd, Castle Place, 166 High Street, Lewes, East Sussex, BN7 1XU, UK. Copyright in the Work © GMC Publications Ltd, 2024. ISBN 9781787081789. Distributed by Publishers Group West in the United States. All rights reserved. No part of this publication may be reproduced, stored in a retrieval system, or transmitted in any form or by any means without the prior permission of the publisher and copyright owner. While every effort has been made to obtain permission from the copyright holders for all material used in this book, the publishers will be pleased to hear from anyone who has not been appropriately acknowledged and to make the correction in future reprints. The publishers and authors can accept no legal responsibility for any consequences arising from the application of information, advice, or instructions given in this publication. A catalogue record for this book is available from the British Library. Editorial: Sam Taylor, Susie Duff, Robert Hiley, Lauren Jarvis, Vivienne Button, Rachel Roberts, Steve White, Vincent Vincent, Ziggy Opoczynska, Nick Pierce. Design: Tim Lambert, Jo Chapman, Emily Hurlock. Publisher: Jonathan Grogan. Production: Jim Bulley. Photos: Shutterstock.com Illustrations: Michelle Urra, Sara Thielker, Alex Bailey. Special thanks: Joe Williams. Colour origination by GMC Reprographics. Printed and bound in China.